922.22
BER

Novitiate Library
Mont La Salle
Napa, California

BERNARD
OF
CLAIRVAUX

Other books by Father M. Basil Pennington

MONASTERY

LAST OF THE FATHERS

THE CISTERCIAN SPIRIT

RULE AND LIFE

CONTEMPLATIVE COMMUNITY

THE MONASTIC WAY

LIGHT FROM THE CLOISTER

THE WAY OF THE CISTERCIANS

MONASTIC JOURNEY TO INDIA

JUBILEE:
A Monk's Journal

O HOLY MOUNTAIN:
Journal of a Retreat on Mount Athos

IN SEARCH OF TRUE WISDOM:
Visits to Eastern Spiritual Fathers and Mothers

THOMAS MERTON, BROTHER MONK:
The Quest for True Freedom

THROUGH THE YEAR WITH THE SAINTS:
A Daily Companion for Private or Liturgical Prayer

BERNARD OF CLAIRVAUX

A Saint's Life in Word and Image

M. Basil Pennington, O.C.S.O.
Dr. Yael Katzir
Ned Johnston, Photographer

Our Sunday Visitor Publishing Division
Our Sunday Visitor, Inc.
Huntington, Indiana 46750

The translations of the works of Bernard of Clairvaux used here, when they are not those of the author/compilers, are taken from *The Works of Bernard of Clairvaux*, Cistercian Fathers Series, published by Cistercian Publications, Kalamazoo, MI 49008.

The illustrations in this book, unless otherwise credited, are courtesy of Ned Johnston.

Copyright © 1994 by Our Sunday Visitor Publishing Division, Our Sunday Visitor, Inc.

All rights reserved. With the exception of short excerpts for critical reviews, no part of this book may be reproduced in any manner whatsoever without permission in writing from the publisher. Write:
Our Sunday Visitor Publishing Division
Our Sunday Visitor, Inc.
200 Noll Plaza
Huntington, Indiana 46750

International Standard Book Number: 0-87973-467-1
Library of Congress Catalog Card Number: 93-83255

Cover design by Monica Watts

PRINTED IN THE UNITED STATES OF AMERICA

CONTENTS

Introduction • 7

1 • Finding the Way • 13

2 • The Monastic Way • 37

3 • A Pilgrim on the Road to the Heavenly Jerusalem • 75

4 • A Voice at the Crossroads for the Church • 141

5 • Walking Through His Own Times • 197

6 • At Journey's End • 231

Epilogue • 249

Chronology • 255

Select Bibliography • 256

Introduction

There have been many books published about Bernard of Clairvaux, but there has never been one quite like this, nor with precisely the same purpose.

The significance of Bernard is more than hinted at by the fact that recently his nine hundredth birthday was celebrated throughout the world from Kalamazoo, Michigan, to Pretoria, South Africa; from Australia to Rome. The historian though is more apt to point to the twelfth century and especially to the first half of that century.

There is hardly a page of it that is not touched by this man who sought to step out of history and found himself at the very heart of his times. There were, of course, other very significant men and women who shared that century with Bernard, but no other is so present to us. This is in part due to the magnificent, rich literary heritage the Abbot of Clairvaux took care to leave us. More intrinsically and effectively it is so because Bernard stood at the crossroads and gave direction to the future, a future that still lives in us.

The student, looking at the twenty-one-year-old Bernard, asks himself: How did this young man exercise such leadership in his family and then in his chosen career? How was he able to go on to become a leader not only of his own monastic order but of the whole of the monastic order, of the whole Roman Church, of western society? Wherein lies his power? Some of us know Bernard primarily as a spiritual master and we ask: How did his quest for a deep life in the Spirit, his turning his back on all that his social position offered, his choice of the smallest, poorest, most hidden of monasteries, and his fierce dedication to asceticism and mysticism lead to his becoming such a powerful force for renewal within society as a whole, even while he turned down the ecclesiastical preferment he might have honorably accepted? What is the answer to these questions?

Is it that this person who so frequently signed himself "Abbot of Clairvaux" never allowed himself to be co-opted by a role? He bewailed how little he filled out the accepted image of abbot — "O abbot and abbot!" — yet he consistently and resolutely decided to be the "chimaera" that he was and to refuse no legitimate call to give who he was. Through his own writings, expressions of himself — both his more personal letters and his carefully polished treatises — in the following pages we are going to allow Bernard to reveal himself.

We cannot hope to understand Bernard the person, as any other person, outside the context within which he lived, moved, and had his being. The moments of his life intersected with the ongoing hours of history, the moments of his century. Bernard is fully a man of his times, that is why he was able to so fully impact upon his times even as they formed the forward thrust that ultimately formed our own times. Bernard knew what stirred in the hearts and hopes of the men and women of his times because they stirred in his own heart and he was deeply in touch with his own heart.

This volume is unique because it invites you, the reader, to walk with a great man, a great human being, on life's journey — his life's journey, which is unique and powerful, and yet is, like yours and mine, so very human.

This volume invites us to walk on that journey not as it is seen through the eyes of later historians but as Bernard himself lived it and shared it. We bring together here, along with Bernard's own words and sharing, the images of his times: the architecture he so loved and which spoke so powerfully to him; the manuscripts — how concerned he was about their careful execution and artful but nondistracting ornamentation; and the sculptures and frescoes, which give us a multidimensional experience of the world with which he so passionately interacted.

We seek here — and herein lies another aspect that makes this volume unique — to make no judgments (though this is difficult because one easily becomes personally involved with Bernard). We want to leave it to you, the reader, to face your own questions and to perhaps find some answers through an intimate yet objective look at the unfolding of this complex personality.

We offer a chronology of Bernard's life, indicating where his various literary works came forth. Unfortunately it is most difficult to date more than a relatively few of his letters. The chapters of this volume will mark the major stages or milestones on Bernard's journey. A brief introduction to each will seek to situate Bernard's moment in its historical hour.

In the following pages we want to let Bernard speak for himself. Not so much recounting the historical facts, which we have briefly set forth in the introductions, but rather telling us what they meant for him, what they were trying to express.

Bernard of Clairvaux is in some ways difficult to read. Nine centuries separate us from him. The clock of history has moved on. There is certainly a great cultural difference. Moreover, we will be reading Bernard in translation. This creates its own problems as well as depriving us of much of the beauty of his poetic prose with its rich tonalities. Bernard's almost constant use of Scripture to express his ideas is certainly something foreign to us. Especially in that most of the time he is not employing the more direct and obvious historical or literal sense of the Scriptures but rather the spiritual or mystical sense that was so popular in his times.

A single text can bear many such senses, and Bernard revels in this richness. Again, his very profuse use of symbolism can be bewildering. However, the use of the symbolic is a value that is being rediscovered in our own times as we move beyond the rationalism of the printed word to more comprehensive media forms. Familiarity with Bernard can help us in recovering this richer form of human communication.

It has been a joy working together preparing this volume. We thank all those who have assisted us along the way, especially Ned Johnston, our photographer; Otto Grundler, Director of the Medieval Institute at Western Michigan University; and E. Rozanne Elder, Director of the Institute of Cistercian Studies at the same university. May you enjoy walking for a bit with Bernard of Clairvaux and in the walking discover more deeply the resources that dwell within you.

◆ ONE

Finding the Way

Bernard himself came from a very fine family. His father was Tescelin, Châtelain of Fontaines, a stronghold overlooking the main road to the near Burgundian town of Dijon. His mother, Aleth, was a Montbard, an even more noble family, whose uncle was the Duke of Burgundy. Bernard was born in 1090 at the family home, Fontaines-les-Dijon.

Bernard grew up privileged among five brothers and a sister. If history does not give us the details, his later writings certainly prove he received an excellent education. Through the long years of his

A restored seventeenth-century tower at the authentic location of Bernard's birthplace in Fontaines-les-Dijon, Burgundy, France.

A twelfth- to thirteenth-century commemorative chapel to St. Bernard in Fontaines-les-Dijon. Many people come here for prayer and marital ceremonies.

adolescence, while his brothers were jousting and becoming knights he must have been devoting himself earnestly to his studies. Nonetheless, he imbibed the values of his class, the marks of chivalry, even if he was to give them a sublimated expression: a prowess to fight for the Church and for justice and peace, wielding with incomparable skill and courage the sword of rhetoric; an exquisite fidelity to the Church and to the Order that he served and to his many friends; a largesse that saw no limits in the way he gave himself to all in need; and a courtly love for a divine Spouse and for his Lady, the holy virgin Mary.

He was twenty-one, in 1112, old for those times, before he came to a decision about his path in life. He had ample time to see what the Church might offer him by way of ecclesiastical preferment. Most of the ambitious young clerics who studied with him had their eyes on these and gossiped freely about them. His brothers and his life at Fontaines-les-Dijon told him all he needed to know about the possibilities open to him if he opted to follow in his father's footsteps. He would in fact always belong to the clergy and the nobility, but in his own unique way he would bring these two classes to live in him in harmony with the other class in this three-tiered society. He would join a community of brothers who would live and labor like peasants.

Bernard's eyes turned toward one of the new reformed monasteries, a little one not far from his home. Cîteaux, which was then called the New Monastery, was located about twenty miles south of Fontaines-les-Dijon. There, among woodlands and marshes, twenty-one monks from the flourishing abbey of Molesme had settled in 1098. Some of the founders returned to Molesme with their leader, the saintly Abbot Robert. But Alberic, his prior, who died in 1109, and Stephen Harding and others of the original group stayed, and they were gradually joined by new recruits.

This hunting scene is typical of the knightly class. Illuminated manuscript, twelfth century, Cîteaux, Burgundy. Opening illumination to the *Moralia in Job*. (Dijon Municipal Library)

Above: The old building of the Cistercian monastery at Cîteaux that remained from the Middle Ages.
Below: Wild marshes around Cîteaux. Bernard chose to live a life of austere monasticism in the wilderness.

Cîteaux was still the New Monastery, something of an experiment, when it captured Bernard's heart and won his allegiance. Here he could indeed be hidden away and in a way hide from some of the things that enkindled consuming ambitions in the human heart. In the silence and solitude he could go deeper into that heart and get in touch with its truer aspirations, its longing for the divine and for the things that last beyond this ephemeral life, this life so cheaply bartered for a bit of glory in jousts and petty wars.

Bernard would not set out on his journey to Cîteaux alone. Here this remarkable young man's quality as leader begins to show forth. Once he decided that joining the small obscure monastery of Cîteaux was the best path, he was not content to follow it alone. He sought to draw along with him all whom he loved. And he succeeded, to the extent of leading thirty-two relatives and friends to the gates of Cîteaux, including all his married brothers — their wives went off to nunneries. His youngest brother, still too young to enter the cloister, and his father, like many others, would follow later.

We are told that as he came into manhood Bernard constantly questioned himself on the meaning of his life: "Bernarde, ut quid venisti?" — Bernard, for what have you come? Why do you exist? Confronted with the smallness and selfishness that trivializes our lives, we all look for the greater meaning. We seek to escape our meanness.

The fountain of mercy . . . is common to all, "for in many things we all offend," and consequently have need of the fountain of mercy to wash away the defilement of our transgressions. "All have sinned," says the Apostle, "and need the glory, that is, the mercy of God"; and to whichever order we may belong, whether we are prelates, virgins or married, "if we say we have no sin, we deceive ourselves and the truth is not in us." Therefore, since "no one is free from stain," the fountain of mercy is necessary for all alike. . . .
Sermons for the Nativity of the Lord, 1.7

A fountain in the cloister of the Cistercian Monastery of Notre Dame, Le Thoronet, France. Founded in 1146.

Bernard began to see the folly of many of the worldly pursuits that so engrossed those around him at Fontaines-les-Dijon.

The wicked therefore walk around in circles, naturally wanting whatever will satisfy their desires, yet foolishly rejecting that which would lead them to their true end, which is not in consumerism but in consummation. Hence they exhaust themselves in vain instead of perfecting their lives seeking a blessed end. They take more pleasure in the appearance of things than in their Creator, examining all and wanting to test them one by one before trying to reach the Lord of the universe.... This is altogether impossible because life is too short, our strength too weak, competition too keen; we are too fatigued by the long road and vain efforts. I am speaking of us who exchanged our glory for the likeness of a calf that eats grass, who have become by sin like irrational beasts.

If I owe all for having been created, what can I add for being remade, and being remade in the way I have been? It was less easy to remake me than to make me. It was written not only about me, but of every created being: "He spoke and they were made." But he who made me by a single word, in remaking me had to speak many words, work miracles, suffer hardships and not only hardships but even unjust treatment. "What shall I render to the Lord for all that he has given me?" In his first work he gave me myself, in his second work he gave me himself, when he gave me himself he gave me back myself. Given and re-given, I owe myself twice over. What can I give God in return for himself? Even if I give him myself a thousand times, what am I to God?

On Loving God, 15-20

Bernard saw, too, the vanity and ambition of many of those who had chosen to pursue an ecclesiastical career.

Promoted to honor over the possessions of the Lord, they pay the Lord no honor. Hence that bogus splendor that you see every day, that theatrical ap-

A twelfth-century bishop's palace that stands adjacent to the Cathedral in Laon, France.

parel, that regal pomp. Hence the gold embossments on their bridles, on their saddles, on their spurs — spurs that carry more costly adornment than their altars.

Hence the heavily laden tables with their glittering glassware, the carousing and drunkenness, the music of harp and lyre and flute, the vats overflowing with wine, storehouses crammed to the doors and a surplus to be stored elsewhere. Hence the painted casks, the packed money bags. Such is the goal they aim at when they seek a prelacy in the Church, to be deans or archdeacons, bishops or archbishops. Nor do these come to them by way of merit but through works done in the darkness.

On the Song of Songs, 33.15

Above: A view of Laon Cathedral from the West Façade, illustrating the extravagance of town cathedrals in the mid-twelfth century.
Left: Stained-glass window located in Laon Cathedral.

Yet Bernard had a deep and almost dependent attachment to his own family. He gave voice to something of this years later when he wrote a eulogy for his older brother, Girard.

You are aware that a loyal companion has left me alone on the pathway of life; he who was so alert to my needs, so enterprising at work, so agreeable in his ways. Who was ever so necessary to me? Who ever loved me as he? My brother by blood, but bound to me more intimately by religious profession. Share my mourning with me, you who know these things. I was frail in body and he sustained me, faint in heart and he gave me courage, slothful and negligent and he spurred me on, forgetful and improvident and he gave me timely warning. Why was he torn from me? Why snatched from my embraces, a man of one mind with me, a man according to my heart. We loved each other in life. . . .

Our bodily companionship was equally enjoyable to both, because our dispositions were so alike. But only I am wounded by the parting. All that was pleasant we rejoiced to share, now sadness and mourning are mine alone. Anger has swept over me, rage has fastened on me. Both of us were so happy in each other's company, sharing the same experiences, talking together about them. . . .

Girard was mine, so utterly mine. Was

he not mine who was a brother to me by blood, a son by religious profession, a father by his solicitude, my comrade on the spiritual highway, my bosom friend in love? And it is he who has gone from me. I feel it, the wound is deep.

On the Song of Songs, 26.4-9

A monk working in a garden in Cîteaux.

As he reached his twenties Bernard struggled with himself and the alien and conflicting desires that tore him apart within. He heard the imperative call to conversion, a call he in his turn later voiced for the young students of Paris.

And if you want to know, God's will is our conversion. Listen to him then, "Is it my will that the wicked shall die," says the Lord, "and not instead that he should be converted and live?" From these words we realize that there is no true life except in conversion and that there is no other means of entering into life, as the Lord likewise says, "Unless you are converted and become as little children, you shall not enter the kingdom of heaven.". . .

Which of us, brothers, suddenly noticing that the outer garment he wears is stained with filthy spit and soiled with all sorts of dirty stains, does not shudder from head to foot and, hastily tearing it off, throw it aside in disgust? Therefore, anyone who discovers that it is not his clothing that is in such a state should ache all the more and be disturbed in mind because he is putting up with what makes him shudder. The contaminated soul cannot doff itself as easily as it doffs its garments. . . .

Some minds dwell in stew pans, others on purses. The Lord says, "Where your treasure is, there will your heart be also." Is it any wonder that the soul should feel its own wounds so little when it has forgotten who it is and is inwardly estranged from itself, having taken its journey into a far country? Yet there will be a time, coming to itself, it will realize how cruelly it has mutilated itself. . . .

On Conversion, 1-5

Then Bernard continued with even more concrete imagery:

If you have ever seen a man scratching at his hand and rubbing it until it bleeds, then you have a clear picture of a sinful soul. For craving gives way to suffering and mental itching yields to torment. And all the while he was scratching he was well aware that this would happen but he pretended that it would not.

Anyone who has heard the voice of the Lord, "Return, transgressors, to the heart" and has discovered such foul things in his inmost chamber will set out like some detective to investigate them. He will examine each thing and search for the opening by which it filtered in. Close the windows, lock the doors, block up the openings carefully and then when fresh filth has ceased to flow in, you can clean out the old.

As long as a person is without experience in the spiritual combat, he thinks that what is asked of him is easy. But the palate complains of being invited to cheap fare and denied the pleasure of getting drunk. The eyes moan that they are forbidden all titillation. The tongue says, "I have been ordered to restrain myself from story-telling and lies." And yet the eye is not satisfied with seeing nor is the ear sated with hearing.

On Conversion, 5, 7, 8

Once Bernard had made his decision he took about a year to prepare himself — and others, for this intensely attractive and zealous young man would not seize the prize alone — to leave all behind and embrace the path of lifelong conversion. Later writing to a young noble with whose concerns he could readily identify, Bernard gave warning about undue delay.

To his dear friend in Christ, William, greetings from Bernard, Abbot of Clairvaux. Because you show yourself so ready to obey, I must be all the more cautious in what I advise or command you. It is indeed fitting that you should complete as soon as possible the good beginnings of your conversion. Having acted manfully in disdaining your worldly goods, it remains for you to leave yourself as well by living no longer under your own will, to be like a true follower of Christ who became obedient to his Father even unto death and who, when he could do all things, declared that he could do nothing of himself but only as the Father had taught him. As you assure me that the needs of the time, the necessities of the poor and the care of your household seem to forbid this for the time being, I, too, in so far as it rests with me, do not prohibit you from what charity dictates in the matter, providing you do not overstay the time you have set for yourself. I would only warn you not to waste wantonly this liberty which has been conceded to you for a time by following your own whims or even (may such a thing be far from you!) in occupying yourself with secular affairs rather than concerning yourself with the things of God. Farewell.

To William, Count of Nevers, Letter 515

Bernard was not content to attain the blessings of conversion for himself alone. Beginning what would be for him a lifelong practice, with an almost unbelievable magnetism he drew thirty of his relatives to join him. Something of the motivation that drove Bernard in working for the conversion of his relatives can be found in this letter celebrating the conversion of another noble who would one day become the Abbot of Bonneval.

To his very dear son in Christ, Hugh, a new creature in Christ, that he may take courage in the Lord, from Brother Bernard, Abbot of Clairvaux.

When I heard the good news of your conversion, my heart was filled with joy. It is a cause of joy for humans and angels. Already it is a festal day in heaven, a day resounding with songs of praise and thanksgiving. A noble youth, gently nurtured, has conquered the evil one, scorned the world, sacrificed his body, renounced the affection of his parents and taking to himself wings, leaped over the snares of riches.

Whence such wisdom, my son? Not even among the ancients of Babylon was such wisdom found. They were those who, according to or rather against the teaching of the Apostle, wished to become rich and fell into temptation, the devil's snare for them. But the wisdom of my Hugh is of heaven and not of this world. "I give you praise, Father, that you have hidden all this from the wise and revealed it to a child." Do you also, my son, thank our Redeemer for his gift to you and keep the innocence of a child with the thoughts of grown-ups? Do not let the roughness of our life frighten your tender years. The sweetness of Christ will take the bitterness from the Prophet's broth. If you feel the stings of temptation, lift your eyes to the serpent on the staff and draw life from the wounds of Christ. He will be your mother and you will be his son. The nails which cleave his hands and feet must also pass through yours.

But a person's household are his worst enemies. These are they who love not you but the satisfaction they derive from you. But let them hear from you those words, "If you really love me, you would be glad that I am on my way to my Father." And now hear what St. Jerome says, "If your mother should lie prostrate at the door, if she should bare her breasts, the breasts that gave you suck, if your nephew should be hanging on your neck, yet with dry eyes fixed upon the cross, go ahead and tread over your prostrate mother and father. It is the height of piety to be cruel for Christ's sake." Do not be moved by the tears of demented parents who weep because from being a child of wrath you have become a child of God. Why have these unhappy people sentiments so harsh? What cruel love, what mistaken affection is theirs!

Bad company, it is said, corrupts noble minds. So I advise you, my son, to avoid as far as you can idle talking with guests. It only fills the ears without filling the mind. Learn to pray, to lift up your heart to God, your eyes in supplication to heaven. It is an impossible thing to believe that God could ever close his heart to you or be deaf to your cries and sighs.

For the rest, remember always and in everything to obey the counsels of your spiritual fathers as well as the commandments of the Divine Majesty. Do this and you shall live. Do this and a rich blessing shall come upon you so that for every single thing you have left you will receive a hundredfold in return, even during this life. Do not believe anyone who tries to persuade you that you have been overhasty and would have done better to have waited until you were older. Believe rather him who said, "It is well you should learn to bear the yoke now in your youth."

Farewell and persevere, for only perseverance is crowned.

Letter 322

Turning from the ways of the world to embrace the monastic way is only the beginning of a long journey of conversion. As an abbot some thirty years later Bernard wrote of his experience:

Those who made me keeper of the vineyard should have taken into account how I had kept my own. For how long a time was it uncultivated and abandoned, reduced to a wilderness. It had failed completely to produce wine, its branches withered without the fruit of virtue because its faith was sterile. Faith was there but it was dead. Without good works how could it be otherwise? That was my life as a layman.

On my conversion to the Lord I began to improve, though very little, not as much I should have. But then, who is fit to do this? Certainly not the holy Prophet who said, "Unless the Lord keeps watch over a city, in vain does the watchperson stand guard." What attacks I remember being exposed to from him who shoots arrows at the innocent from cover! O my vineyard, what an amount of produce was robbed from me by subtle trickery at the very time when I was growing more vigilant in my care of you. How many and how precious were the clusters of good works that were blighted by anger or snatched away by boasting or defiled by vainglory. What temptations did I not endure from gluttony, from mental sloth-

fulness, from pusillanimity of spirit and the storm of passion. Such was my state and yet they made me the keeper of the vineyard, failing to consider what I was doing or had done with my own nor listening to the voice of the teacher who said, "If a man does not know how to manage his own household, how can he care for God's Church?"
On the Song of Songs, 30.6

There is undoubtedly some rhetorical exaggeration in what Bernard says of himself. Conversion is not always from evil to good; it is sometimes from good to better.

There is one thing you have done at which everyone marvels. It is that, although your lives were holy, you thought nothing of this but made it your business to share the holy lives of others that yours might become yet more holy. It is so rare that anyone leading a good life is ready to do this that when it happens everyone admires it.
To the Monks of Alps, Letter 142.2

When some of the monks of the Abbey of St. Mary at York sought to pursue a deeper conversion, leaving their rather lax monastery to embrace a more fervent life at the new Cistercian abbey of Fountains, their old abbot, Dom Geoffrey, claimed their departure would cause scandal. Bernard was not slow in replying.

One must distinguish between different sorts of scandal. Carnal affections must be cut off completely for the love of Christ. The Gospels thunder exceedingly, the whole of Scripture cries out on every page that worldly advantage must be abandoned for the good of the soul. To ignore this is not only wrong, it is almost heretical. I am not at all sure that such a return as you hope for [Abbot Geoffrey wanted his monks to return from Fountains] ought not to be regarded as a grave sin. It is a most dangerous thing, not far short from a catastrophe, to presume on the mercy of God at the expense of his justice and, as it were, to play one off against the other or in the words of Scripture "to add sin to sin and say, 'The mercy of God is great.'" It is a mistaken sort of discretion to put small things before great and to place the worse on the same footing as the better.

Letter 94

It was this ongoing conversion, this conversion from good to better, that Bernard would largely inspire and foster throughout the monastic order.

◆TWO

The Monastic Way

We have all seen pictures or even statues of Bernard of Clairvaux. They appear in books recounting the history of the Middle Ages. They are found in churches and art galleries.

Bernard does not usually appear in the rich apparel of priest or prelate, priest and prelate though he was. He wears the long gray-white cowl of the monk, rough wool from the back of a sheep, washed, woven, and worn. It bespeaks simplicity, poverty, and purity. When its ample sleeves are

A fourteenth-century statue of St. Bernard in the Parish Church, Fontaines-les-Dijon.

These vineyards belong to the Monastery of Cîteaux and are situated near Clos Vougeot in Burgundy. The twelfth-century wine cellars (background) are still standing.

stretched out it takes the form of a cross, reminding the monk that he has committed himself to take up his cross daily and follow Christ the crucified. It will one day be his shroud, worn daily to tell the monk that he has indeed already died to this world. He has entered the *paradisus claustralis*, the paradise of the cloister, a little bit of this earth set apart for the things of heaven. He has chosen to go apart. He lives on the fringe — not the outer fringe but the inner fringe, at the heart of the world and more particularly of the Church, which is at the heart of the world. But Bernard is more than a monk. He holds a crosier, a shepherd's crook. He is a shepherd of monks, an abbot. At the age of twenty-five, in 1115, after only three years in the cloister, this gifted young man was sent forth to create a new cloister. From Cîteaux he led twelve into the Valley of Bitterness and changed it into the Valley of Light: Clairvaux.

It was the beginning of an enormous procession; Clairvaux would shed its light upon the whole Christian world. Thousands would come and Bernard would spend the remaining thirty-eight years of his short life shepherding them. As shepherd he would feed them a rich spiritual fare that would continue to nourish through the succeeding centuries. Bernard is perhaps before all and above all, at least in relation to others, a teacher, an abbot — *abba*, father.

When we look upon the face of a great clock there are moments when the minute hand seems to prevail, completely overshadowing that which bespeaks the hour. But the hour prevails. Bernard was a man of his time and his culture and his class. Gifted by nature and grace he reached deeply into the heart and saw clearly what is there. The revelation that came through Christ Jesus illuminated his life and thinking. Yet he belonged to his hour of history.

If the beginning of the twelfth century was a time when the juices of society were in rapid ferment, the same was true of the Church. The renewal authoritatively set underway by the audacious and adroit monk Hildebrand, Pope Gregory VII, was bucking its way through established bureaucracies and political ambitions. Its most striking expressions were the little monastic establishments cropping up everywhere: men and women daring to embrace radical reform and believing it was important enough to make it worthwhile to let go of everything else.

During the first half of the twelfth century the clock of history moved through some very significant moments when old and emerging clashed.

The great Abbey of Cluny, with its two thousand dependencies of various sorts, represented the Church that was passing.

It was a Church that co-opted the splendor of the imperial court and the financial support of the sinful, high feudal nobility. It

Above: Basilica of the Cluniac Abbey of the Holy Heart (exterior view), Paray le Monial, France, twelfth century.
Below: Basilica of the Cluniac Abbey of the Holy Heart (note the decoration detail).

sought to portray heaven on earth, to make the transcendent immanent within the liturgy and ritual of church and cloister. It was a noble thing and welcomed the noble class. It employed the lower classes and lived off the labor of serfs.

The new emerging monasticism was far more earthy. The monks worked in the soil, earning their bread by the sweat of their brow. They welcomed laborers and serfs into their ranks. If hierarchy in some ways prevailed — for one had virtually to be a cleric to receive the education necessary to be a choir monk — nonetheless, nobles became lay brothers and all lived and labored together as brothers. Time for labor and time for contemplation left little time for splendid liturgies. Simplicity prevailed. The renewal of the contemplative quest that sought divine espousals co-opted the chivalrous romanticism of courtly love that fired men's imaginations and directed their lives. A new, higher adventure was offered, one that promised unending rewards and happiness.

Bernard became the incarnation as well as the spokesman for this renewal in monastic garb. His rhetoric was his sword. And it prevailed. Though Cluny and those influenced by its spirit tried to renew (there was a Benedictine chapter at Reims [1128] and Peter the Venerable, the Abbot of Cluny, issued reform statutes), Bernard's *Apologia* (1125) opened the way for it to be supplanted. Bernard's *Apologia*, one of the most popular writings of this time, gave high praise to all that was good at Cluny even as it cut the ground out from under it with powerful rhetorical irony.

The monastic dimension of Bernard's reforming zeal reached beyond the cloister to embrace in a wholly new way the knightly order from which he had sprung. In response to a perceived need of the times, he fostered a new hybrid. Men of the joust and campaign were encouraged to continue to wield the sword, but now to wield it on behalf of justice and right, in defense of Church and poor, and to do this in holy obedience. Knights were encouraged to form new orders, to become Knights of the Temple. Their lives would be fortified and consecrated by vows like those of monks. The fortress would become a monastery while still remaining a fortress. The Templar would continue to be a warrior, fighting to gain and preserve the freedom of the holy places and the safety of the pilgrims going to them. Yet their peaceful hours in the fortress would not be unlike those of a monk in his monastery.

Bernard the idealist saw his Clairvaux as the heavenly Jerusalem, the holy city come down from above. Yet he was a pragmatist, very much in touch with reality. Those he could not lure to the cloister he challenged and encouraged to bring heaven to earth, to bring the peace of the cloister into the world.

Bernard found the origins of the monastic way in the very origins of the Church.

The monastic order was the first order in the Church, it was out of it that the Church developed. In all the earth there was nothing more like the angelic orders, nothing closer to the heavenly Jerusalem, our mother, because of the beauty of its chastity and the fervor of its love. The Apostles were its moderators and its members were those whom Paul often calls "the saints." It was their practice to keep nothing as private property, for, as it is written, "distribution was made to each as he had need."

Apologia, 24

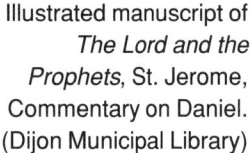

Illustrated manuscript of *The Lord and the Prophets*, St. Jerome, Commentary on Daniel. (Dijon Municipal Library)

Bernard had a clear understanding of the way of life, which he embraced in coming to Cîteaux.

Our way of life is an awareness of our need, it is humility, it is voluntary poverty, obedience, peace, joy in the Holy Spirit. Our way of life means being under a Master, under an abbot, under a rule, under discipline. Our way of life means applying ourselves to silence, being trained in fasts, vigils, prayers, and manual labor. Above all, it means clinging to that most excellent way which is charity, and furthermore, advancing day by day in these things and persevering in them until the last day.
To the Monks of Alps, Letter 142.1

"The just man in the arms of Abraham." A façade at the Benedictine Abbey in St. Foy, Conques, France.

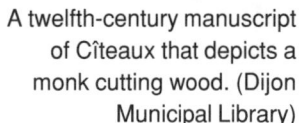

A twelfth-century manuscript of Cîteaux that depicts a monk cutting wood. (Dijon Municipal Library)

Bernard evidently remained always excited about his vocation. After years in the monastic life he could still write:

> Oh, if only you knew, if only I could explain to you! If you could but taste for a moment the full ears of corn on which Jerusalem feasts. If I could but have you as my fellow in the school of piety of which Jesus is the master! How gladly would I share with you the warm loaves which, still piping hot, fresh, as it were, from the oven, Christ in his heavenly bounty so often breaks with the poor!
>
> Believe me who have experience, you will find much more when laboring among woods than you ever will among books. Woods and stones will teach you what you can never hear from any master. Do you imagine you cannot suck honey from the rocks and oil from the hardest stone; that the mountains do not drop sweetness and the hills flow with milk and honey, that the valleys are not filled with corn? So many things occur to me that I cannot restrain myself.
>
> *To Henry Murdac, Letter 106.28*

Bernard saw entering monastic life as truly a new beginning, a second baptism.

Fountain at the Abbey of Fontenay.

You have also asked my opinion on monastic profession as a second baptism. Why has our way of life rather than other penitential callings merited the prerogative of this appellation? I think it is because of the more perfect renouncement of the world and the singular excellence of such a spiritual way of life. It makes those who live it and love it stand out from others as rivals of the angels

and as hardly human at all; for it restores the divine image in the human soul and makes us Christlike, much as baptism does. It is also like another baptism in that we mortify the earthly side of our nature, so that we may be more and more clothed with Christ, being thus again "buried in the likeness of his death." Just as in baptism we are delivered from the power of darkness and carried over into the kingdom of light, so likewise in the second regeneration of this holy profession we are refashioned in the light of virtue, being delivered, not now from the unique darkness of original sin, but from many actual sins. . . .
On Precept and Dispensation, 54

Bernard had a profound reverence for the monasticism that commonly flourished in his time, that which flowed from the Cluniac reform of the tenth century. Cluny was founded in 909, was blessed with a series of long-lived, fervent abbots, and was protected by a papal privilege that exempted all its houses from the jurisdiction of the local bishops.

No one has ever seen me denouncing this Order or murmuring against it. I am always delighted to see any of Cluny's members. I receive them with all due honor. I converse with them respectfully and encourage them in all humility.... This way of life is holy and good. Chastity is its adornment, discretion its crown. Organized by the Fathers and predestined by the Holy Spirit, it is eminently suited for the saving of souls. ... I have asked them to pray for me. I have attended their community meetings. I have spoken a good deal with many of them about the Bible and the salvation of souls, both publicly in chapter and privately. I have never secretly or openly encouraged anyone to leave that Order and come to ours. In fact, I have rebuffed many monks who wanted to come and if any came knocking, I turned them away....
Apologia, 4

Yet he could not accept the abuses that had unfortunately become common among the Cluniac monks. Their fervor had attracted generous donations giving many of the abbeys burdensome wealth. In their zeal for the Opus Dei, the Work of God, the Cluniacs had multiplied public services in Church to the extent of all but eliminating personal prayer and manual labor. The centralization of authority at Cluny, contrary to the local autonomy postulated by the Rule of St. Benedict, made it difficult to maintain discipline in the hundreds of monasteries spread throughout Europe.

It is said correctly that it was by holy Fathers that this way of life was organized: they did not abrogate the Rule, they merely moderated its severity on account of the weak, so that more men might be saved. At the same time, I would hate to think that these holy Fathers would have commanded or allowed the many foolish excesses I have noticed in several monasteries. I am astonished that monks could be so lacking in moderation in matters of food and drink and with respect to clothing and bedding, carriages and buildings. Things have come to such a pass that right order and religion are thought to be promoted, the more concern and pleasure and enthusiasm there is regarding such things.

Abstemiousness is accounted miserliness, sobriety strictness, silence gloom. On the other hand laxity is labeled discretion, extravagance generosity, talkativeness sociability and laughter joy. Fine clothes and costly caparisons are regarded as mere respectability and being fussy about bedding is hygiene. When they lavish these things on one another, they call it love. Such love undermines true love. Such discretion disgraces real discretion. This sort of kindness is full of cruelty, for it so looks after the body that the soul is strangled.

These are only small things. I am coming to things of greater moment. I merely mention these minor details because they happen to be rather common. I shall say nothing about the soaring heights and extravagant lengths and unnecessary widths of the churches, nothing about their expensive decoration and their novel images, which catch the attention of those who go in to pray and dry up their devotion.

Oh, vanity of vanities, whose vanity is rivalled only by its insanity! The walls of the church are aglow but the poor of the Church go hungry. The stones of the church are covered with gold while its children are left naked. The food of the poor is taken to feed the eyes of the

The Church of the Abbey of St. Mary Magdalene in Vézelay, France, twelfth century.

Above (left): *The Death of the Miser* (capital). While the miser's soul is departing through his mouth into the grip of two demons, two serpents attack the money under his bed. Vézelay, twelfth century.
Above (right): *The Legend of Saint Benedict* (capital). While a demon is trying to tempt a woman, St. Benedict is giving her his blessing. Vézelay, twelfth century.
Below: *Nymph Shot by a Centaur* (capital). Church of St. Peter, Priory of Cluny in Souvigny, France, twelfth century.

rich and amusement is provided for the curious while the needy have not even the necessities of life.

What excuse can there be for these ridiculous monstrosities in the cloisters where the monks do their reading, extraordinary things at once beautiful and ugly?

Here we find filthy monkeys and fierce lions, fearful centaurs, harpies and striped tigers, soldiers at war and hunters blowing their horns.

Here is one head with many bodies, there is one body with many heads.

Over there is a bust with a serpent for its tail, a fish with an animal's head and a creature that is horse in front and goat behind and a second beast with horns and the rear of a horse.

All around there is such an amazing variety of shapes that one could easily prefer to take one's reading from the walls instead of from a book. One could spend the whole day gazing fascinated at these things, one by one, instead of meditating on the law of God. Good Lord, even if the foolishness of it all occasions no shame, at least one might balk at the expense.

There are plenty of other things that could be added.

Apologia, 16ff

St. Bernard was indeed not the founder of the Cistercian Order, but he was the architect of its expansion and success. In the twelfth-century monastic movement, the Cistercians introduced a reform that

Imaginary Animals (capital). Cluniac Abbey, Mozac, France, twelfth century.

Eberbach, a Cistercian monastery in the German Rhineland, where St. Bernard visited in 1136.

changed the accents on the emphasis of the prevailing Cluniac example. The Cluniacs stressed the prayers as the ultimate, most sublime goal of the monk. The Cistercians juxtaposed a far more rigid and austere ideal. Under the slogan of "pray and work" (*ora et labora*), they have adopted manual work as a part of the monastic routine. St. Bernard had given manual work a higher meaning (significance) as he propagated (preached) work as a purifying element. One has to understand that, in those days, the people who came to the monastery from the nobility, like Bernard, did not know how to work but also were forbidden to do so. Work was for the peasants.

What characterized the Cistercians was the fact that they were a pioneer order that wished to revive the monastic ideal of withdrawal from society as well as the spiritual concept of the desert. Unlike the Cluniacs who became big feudal lords located mostly on top of the hills like the feudal castles, the Cistercians went into the woods, which in Europe were like the eastern deserts, and did a lot of wood-clearing. They sat in the valleys and started to use hydraulic power. They dried some marshes by digging canals and were among the first

Above: A capital in the Cloister of Fontenay, illustrating the puritan Cistercian architecture.
Below: Another example of the puritan Cistercian architecture in the Cloister of Notre Dame, Le Thoronet.

to introduce the water mills in their lands. The water became a very prominent element as well as image in the Cistercian life.

More than anyone else, St. Bernard applied the concept of "cistercian austerity" also to the Cistercian architecture. He applied the concept of austerity and shaped the architecture of the Cistercian Order in his time and beyond. We are not Cluniacs. We want it simple, functional, and austere. It is very remarkable to see how similar in shape are all the Cistercian monasteries of the twelfth century.

Above: A monk harvesting the crops. Manuscript of Cîteaux, twelfth century.
Facing page: A monk drying the marshes and clearing the wood in the lands of Cîteaux.
Below: Monks harvesting grapes. Manuscript of Cîteaux, twelfth century.

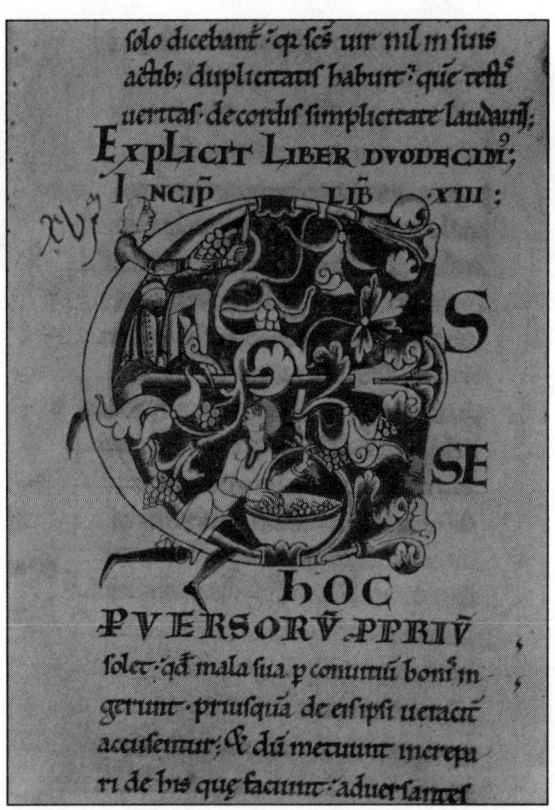

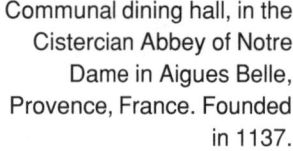

Communal dining hall, in the Cistercian Abbey of Notre Dame in Aigues Belle, Provence, France. Founded in 1137.

Community life, the brethren living together, sharing all and supporting one another on the journey, was a very important dimension of the monastic way for Bernard of Clairvaux. He wrote of it in glowing terms in his letters and sermons.

The Cistercian family welcomed you with open arms and the angels looked down upon you with smiling faces. They know very well what pleases God more than anything is familial concord and unity since the Prophet says, "Gracious is the sight and full of comfort when brothers and sisters dwell together in unity" and again, "When sibling helps sibling, theirs is the strength of a fortress."

To the Monks of Alps, Letter 142.2

It is a glorious thing for men to dwell in one house with one mind. How good and how pleasant to see brothers living in unity! You can see one lamenting his sins, another praising God; this one min-

istering to all, another teaching and instructing; this one praying, that one reading. One confesses his sins, another does penance for his. One shines for his charity, another for his humility. One can be seen to be humble in prosperity, another patient in adversity. This one is engaged in work, another rests in contemplation. Thus we can say truly this is the camp of God; this is an awesome place. It is none other than the house of God and the gate of heaven.
Occasional Sermon, 42.2

You, my brothers, if you willingly share with us your brethren the gifts you have received from above, if you show yourself everywhere among us obliging, affectionate, graceful, obedient and humble, you also shall receive the testimony of all that you, too, are redolent with the best of ointments. Yes, every one among you, my brothers, who not only supports with patience the corporal and spiritual infirmities of his brother but insofar as he is permitted and has power assists him by kind services, comforts him by his words and directs him by his counsels or, if the Rule will not allow for this, consoles the weak one at least by his fervent and incessant prayer — every such brother, I say, exhales a good odor in his community and smells sweet with the best ointments.
On the Song of Songs, 12.5

Bernard did not have much sympathy for the eremitical life. He saw only its weaknesses and contrasted them with the strengths of the community life. Thus he writes to a nun who is thinking about withdrawing from her community to live a more solitary life:

For anyone wishing to lead a bad life the desert supplies ample opportunity. The woods afford cover, and solitude assures silence. No one can censure the evil no one sees. Where there is no fear of blame the tempter approaches more boldly and evil is committed with greater freedom. In a convent, if you would do good, there is no one to stop you; if you would do evil, you are not able. Soon everyone would know about it, it would soon be blamed and corrected just as on the other hand all would admire, respect and imitate the good they saw. Therefore you see, my daughter, that in a convent greater glory awards your deserts and a more prompt correction your faults, for among others you set an example by a good life and give offence by a bad one. . . .

The wolf lurks in the woods. If you, a little sheep, penetrate the shadows of the woods alone, you are offering yourself as a prey to the wolf. But listen to me, daughter, listen to a faithful counsel. Whether you are a saint or a sinner do not cut yourself off from the flock or you will fall prey to the wolf and there will be no one to rescue you. If you are a saint, try to edify your sisters by your example.

To a Nun of St. Mary of Troyes, Letter 115, 1-2

Bernard rejoiced to see his sons pass through the different stages of spiritual growth in their monastic communal life. In his series of sermons on the Song of Songs he had occasion to affirm the virtues of the succeeding stages.

Do you see these novices? They came recently, they were converted recently. We cannot say of them that "our vineyard has flowered." It is flowering. What you see appear in them at the moment is the blossom. The time of fruiting has yet to come. Their new way of life, their recent adoption of a better life — these are blossoms. They have assumed a disciplined appearance, a proper deportment in their whole body. What can be seen of them is pleasing, I admit. One notices less attention to painstaking care of the body and of dress; they speak less, their faces are more cheerful, their looks more modest, their movements more correct. But since these are new beginnings, the flowers must be judged by their very novelty and as a promise of fruits rather than as the fruits themselves.

On the Song of Songs, 63.6

Spiritual vineyards signify spiritual men within whom all things are cultivated, all things are germinating, bearing fruit and bringing forth the spirit of salvation.

What was said of the Kingdom of God we can equally say of these vineyards of the Lord of hosts — that they are within us. We read in the Gospel that the Kingdom will be given to a people who will produce its fruits. St. Paul enumerates these: "The fruits of the Spirit are love, joy, peace, patience, kindness, goodness, forbearance, gentleness, faithfulness, modesty, self-control, chastity." These fruits indicate our progress. They are pleasing to the Bridegroom because he takes care of us.

On the Song of Songs, 63.5

An abbot working in the vineyards at the Cistercian monastery in Latrun, Israel.

Bernard loved his monks tenderly and was deeply affected when, on rare occasions, they defected. Perhaps the most poignant was the defection of his own cousin Robert, a youth who was lured away by the Cluniacs in the earliest days of their controversy with Bernard. In the end Bernard's love prevailed and Robert returned to the Cistercians to live a holy and fruitful life and die a holy death. When Bernard edited his letters for publication, he placed this letter first.

I have said this, my son, not to put you to shame but to help you as a loving father because if you have many masters in Christ, you have few fathers. For, if you will allow me to say so, I begot you in religion by word and example. I nourished you with milk when, while yet a child, it was all you could take. And I would have given you bread if you had waited until you grew up. But alas! how soon and how early were you weaned. Now I fear that all I had cherished with kindness, strengthened with encouragement, confirmed with prayers is even now fading and wasting away. Sadly I weep, not for my lost labor but for the unhappy state of my lost child. Do you prefer that another should rejoice in you who had not labored for you? My case is the same as that of the harlot Solomon judged, whose child was stealthily taken by another who had overlain and killed

her own. You, too, were taken from my side, cut from me. My heart cannot forget you, half of it went with you and what remains cannot but suffer.
 To Robert, Letter 1.10

Bernard the abbot was keenly aware of his duty to teach, even at great cost to himself when he was burdened by many cares and a sickly constitution.

Far from disapproving of those whose purer mind enables them to grasp sublimer truths than I can present, I warmly congratulate them. But expect them to allow me to provide a simpler doctrine for simpler minds. How I wish that all had the gift of teaching! I should be rid of the need to preach these sermons! It is a burden I should like to transfer to another or rather I should prefer that none of you would need to exercise it, that all would be taught by God and that I should have leisure to contemplate God's beauty. Now, however, I must confess, not without tears, that I have no time to seek after God much less to contemplate him, no time to see the king in his beauty seated upon the Cherubim, on a throne raised aloft, to see him in that form in which, as the Father's equal, he was born before the dawning amid the sacred splendors. This is the form in which the angels long to contemplate him forever, God with God. And I, a man, describe him to you according to the human form that he adopted in order to reveal himself with the maximum of esteem and love. Made lower than the angels, he came out of his chambers like a Bridegroom and pitched a tent in the sun. I present him as at-

tractive rather than sublime, as God's appointed servant and not a remote deity, as the one whom the Spirit of the Lord anointed and sent "to bring good news to the poor, to bind up hearts that are broken, to proclaim liberty to captives, freedom to those in prison; to proclaim a year favorable to the Lord."
On the Song of Songs, 22.3

While the abbot's first role is to teach, Bernard had a very full and humane sense of his office. As he wrote to concerned parents:

Knowing that your son is tender and delicate perhaps you are afraid for his health under the harshness of our life. . . . Have comfort. Do not worry. I shall look after him like a father and he will be to me a son until the Father of Mercies, the God of all Consolation, shall receive him from my hands.

I will be for him both a mother and father, both a brother and a sister. I will make the crooked path straight for him and the rough places smooth. I will temper and arrange all things that his soul may advance and his body not suffer. He will serve the Lord with joy and gladness. "His song will be of the Lord's, for great is the glory of the Lord."

To the Parents of Geoffrey of Perrone, Letter 110.2

To another abbot he wrote:

You must remember that you are especially abbot of the sad, fainthearted and discontented among your flock. It is by consoling, encouraging and admonishing that you do your duty and carry your burden and by carrying your burden heal those you carry. If there is anyone so spiritually healthy that he rather helps you than is helped by you, you are not so much his father as his equal, not so much his abbot as his fellow. Why then do you complain that you find the company of some of those who are with you more of a burden than a comfort? You were given them as abbot not to be comforted but to comfort, because you

St. Bernard became a source of encouragement and counsel to many newly established Cistercian communities such as the one that inhabited this cloister at Fontenay.

were the strongest of them all and, by God's grace, able to comfort them all without needing to be comforted by any . . . realize that you hold the place of him who came not to be served but to serve.
To Rainald, Abbot of Foigny, Letter 73.2

For Bernard the ideals of the monastic life were to be carried over as much as possible into lay life as the sure way to salvation. When the idea arose of founding a new order of knighthood that would combine the ideals of the cloister with the military prowess necessary to defend the sacred places in the Holy Land Bernard was eager to support it.

It seems that a new knighthood has recently appeared on the earth and precisely in that part of it which the Orient from on high visited in the flesh. . . . This knighthood ceaselessly wages a twofold war both against flesh and blood and against a spiritual army of evil in the heavens. When someone strongly resists a foe in the flesh, relying solely on the strength of the flesh, I would hardly remark it, since this is common enough. And when war is waged by spiritual strength against vices or demons, that, too, is nothing remarkable, praiseworthy as it is, for the world is full of monks. But when one sees a man of power girding himself with both swords and nobly marking his belt, who would not consider it worthy of all wonder, the more since it has been hitherto unknown? He is truly a fearless knight and secure on every side, for his soul is protected by the armor of faith just as his body is protected by the armor of steel. He is thus doubly armed and need fear neither

Above: The Temple of Solomon (El Aksa Mosque, Temple Mount, Jerusalem) was the site of the headquarters for the Military Order of the Templars. Bernard wrote their Rule at the Church Council of Troyes, France, in 1128.
Below: The Temple of the Lord, known as Templum Domini during the time of the Crusaders, and today as The Dome of the Rock, was the architectural model for the churches built by the Templar Order in Europe.

demons nor men. Not that he fears death — no, he desires it. Why should he fear to live or fear to die when for him to live is Christ and to die is gain? Gladly and faithfully he stands for Christ but he would prefer to be dissolved and to be with Christ, by far the better thing.

Go forth confidently, then, you knights, and repel the foes of the cross of Christ.

In Praise of the New Knighthood, 1

Let us see how these cavaliers of Christ conduct themselves at home as well as in battle. . . . They come and go at the bidding of their superiors. They wear whatever he gives them and do not presume to wear or to eat anything from another source. Thus they shun every excess in clothing and food and content themselves with what is necessary. They live as brothers in a joyful and sober company without wives or children. So that their evangelical perfection will lack nothing, they dwell united in one family with no personal property whatever, careful to keep the unity of the Spirit in the bond of peace. You may say that the whole multitude has but one heart and one soul to the point that nobody follows his own will but rather seeks to follow the commander. . . . I do not know if it would be more appropriate to refer to them as monks or as soldiers, unless perhaps it would be better to recognize them as being both.

In Praise of the New Knighthood, 8

Above: The Church of the Templars. Laon, twelfth century.
Below: *Demons Represent the Enemies of the Believers* (capital). The Templars considered themselves soldiers of Christ who protected the Church against all its enemies. Exterior wall of the Church of the Templars in Laon.

With such defenders and guardians, the Holy City had reason to rejoice. Bernard erupts with poetic enthusiasm.

Rejoice, Jerusalem, and recognize now the time in which you are visited! Be glad and give praise together, wastes of Jerusalem, for the Lord has comforted his people. He has ransomed Jerusalem. The Lord has bared his holy arm in the sight of all peoples. O virgin of Israel, you were fallen and there was none to raise you up. Arise now and shake off the dust, O virgin, captive daughter of Sion. Arise, I say, and stand on high. See the happiness which comes to you from your God.

In Praise of the New Knighthood, 6

Bernard's joy is so deep and so exuberant because for him Jerusalem had meaning far beyond the sacredness of the city that saw the death and resurrection of the Christ.

"Rejoice, Jerusalem, and recognize now the time in which you are visited!" A view of modern Jerusalem from the East.

THREE

A Pilgrim on the Road to the Heavenly Jerusalem

Regard me as God's servant, your brother servant, a companion for your journey to the homeland where we are fellow heirs, if I have loyally fulfilled the service for which I was sent to you, if I have done all I could that you might win the heritage of salvation.

Letter 147

St. Bernard conceived of life as a road symbolic of life's many endless diversions and turning points. In the Middle Ages, people were indeed attracted to roads and took pilgrimages to holy places as expressions of their religious piety or in some cases, penance. The Order of Cluny strongly encouraged this trend. Pilgrimages were generally made to Jerusalem, Rome, and Compostella. However, there were many other holy shrines that attracted people. Some were along the road to Compostella such as Le Puy and Conques. When one looks at European maps, it is easy to notice that the Cluniac monasteries are built along the pilgrim roads. The Cluniacs supervised hostels and provided hospitality for the pilgrims who, in turn, rewarded them with donations. Whereas laymen took pilgrimages, monks took a vow to obey the abbot and observe stability of place. St. Bernard was ferocious in his criticisms of monks, especially those in his own Order who broke with discipline and took to the road — even if the road ended in Jerusalem. With all his rhetoric, he was trying to convince Brother Adam — who broke the discipline of the Order by joining Arnold of Morimond on his pilgrimage to

A sixteenth-century wood sculpture of St. Roch in pilgrim garb.

Jerusalem — to return. The following letter was written to the monk Adam:

Both the humility which I know to be yours as well as the circumstances of danger in which you are placed lend me courage to address you more sharply and rebuke you more freely than I would otherwise do. Who has beguiled you, senseless one, to depart so soon from the salutary resolutions on which you and I, with God our only witness, lately agreed? Do not be foolish, but see that you direct your steps in the way of God's law. Have you forgotten how at Marmoutier you dedicated the first-fruits of your conversion; then how at Foigny you commended yourself to my care, such as it is; how at Morimond you confirmed your stability and then, again on my advice, how you frankly renounced the pilgrimage, or rather vagabondage, suggested by Abbot Arnold, deciding that if he could not lawfully set off, you could not lawfully accompany him? What then? Do you now say that he set off lawfully after all when he went without even waiting for the permission of his superior and left behind such a deplorable scandal among those committed to his care?

Letter 6

Above: On the road to Compostella, the Benedictine monastery in St. Foy, Conques.
Below: Pilgrimages were made to Conques in order to venerate this reliquary of St. Foy.

Although St. Bernard forbids pilgrimages by his own monks, in his rich repertoire of letters and sermons, St. Bernard does allow himself to imagine the emotional and spiritual excitement experienced by the pilgrims who had the chance to venerate Christ in his resting place, the Church of the Holy Sepulchre.

I think that those who are actually able to see with their bodily eyes the bodily resting place of the Lord must experience the strongest of emotions from which they will receive no little profit. Even though this place is now empty of its sacred contents, it remains full of delightful mysteries for us — for us, I say, because it is really our resting place. ... How sweet it must be for pilgrims after the fatigue of their long journey and their many perils on land and sea to find rest there at last — there where they know their own Lord has rested! I should think that in their joy they no longer feel their weariness nor regret their expenses but claim the reward of their labor and the prize of their course according to the words: "They rejoice exceedingly to have found the tomb."

In Praise of the New Knighthood, 29

For monks, this pilgrimage takes place within the monastery where indeed they have already arrived at their Jerusalem. Bernard explains this to the Bishop of Lincoln whose cleric started on a pilgrimage to Jerusalem and instead wished to become a monk of Clairvaux.

I write to tell you that your Philip has found a short way to Jerusalem and has arrived there very quickly. He crossed "the vast ocean stretching wide on every hand" with a favorable wind in a very short time and he has now cast anchor on the shores for which he was making. Even now he stands in the courts of Jerusalem and "whom he heard tidings of in Ephrata he has found in the woodland plains and gladly reverences in the place where he has halted on his journey." He has entered the holy city and has chosen his heritage with them of whom it has been deservedly said, "You are no longer exiles or aliens. The saints are your fellow citizens, you belong to God's household." His going and coming is in their company and he has become one of them, glorifying God and saying with them, "We find our true home in heaven." He is no longer an inquisitive onlooker but a devout inhabitant and an enrolled citizen of Jerusalem — not of that earthly Jerusalem to which Mount Sinai in Arabia is joined and which is in bondage with its children but of that free

Jerusalem which is above and is the mother of us all.

And this, if you want to know, is Clairvaux. It is the Jerusalem united to the one in heaven by whole-hearted devotion, conformity of life and a serene spiritual affinity.

To Bishop Alexander of Lincoln, Letter 64.1-2

Bernard loved the earthly Jerusalem. But this city was, as the Bible clearly set forth, a type or symbol of a new Jerusalem that would come down from above. It was this heavenly Jerusalem that most interested Bernard. And he sought to make that heavenly Jerusalem present on earth in the idealized reality of his Cistercian monasteries.

Dearest brothers, you are walking in the way that leads to life, in the way, direct and undefiled, which leads to the holy city, to "that Jerusalem which is above, which is free, which is our mother." The ascent, I must say, is difficult, seeing as this road runs straight up to the very summit of the mystical mountain. Yet its shortness in comparison with other roads renders it, if not absolutely easy, at any rate the least difficult of all.

Sermons on Various Topics, 22.1

In his first overzealous steps toward reaching his heavenly Jerusalem, the young Bernard all but destroyed his body. His physical health was maimed for the rest of his life. Only the strong hand of authority, that of the Chapter of Abbots and of the Bishop of Châlons, saved for us this man and his brilliant career. As the pilgrim went forward, he learned, too, that not all human passion is immediately subsumed in a great passionate love. It may

The Cloister of Fontenay as a reflection of heavenly Jerusalem on earth.

well be in rich moments of ecstasy. But strong passion leaps out at times in its opposite: anger. Passion, too, affects the judgment and at times, in spite of love, leads to a lack of compassion. Bernard's powerful pen can become a piercing sword. Because of his leadership skills and his love, Bernard was often called forth to be a reconciler. But in his zeal he also at times hurt and evoked enmity toward himself. One way or another, he soon realized that the road to the heavenly Jerusalem is full of obstacles that would need a pilgrimage lasting a lifetime.

Most of his life, Bernard concentrated on the spiritual pilgrimage, which is the vocation of the monk. Many of his sermons are addressed to the various dimensions of the spiritual pilgrimage.

But more important is the pilgrimage of the spirit.

It is a great good to seek God. In my opinion there is no greater blessing. It is the first of gifts and the final stage of our progress. This gift is inferior to none and yields place to none. What could be superior to it, when nothing has a higher place?

It is not with steps of the feet that God is sought but with the desire of the heart. When we happily find him our desire is not quenched but kindled. . . . there will be a fullness of joy but there will be no end to desire and therefore no end to the search.

Think if you can of this eagerness to see God as not caused by his absence, for he is always present. Think of the desire for God without fear of failure, for grace is abundantly present.

On the Song of Songs 84.1

For Bernard, the spiritual journey begins in heaven; God first comes to us so that we might then come to him.

In the beginning God created all things with power and he governed all things with wisdom. Humans had clear evidence of the divine power and wisdom in the creation and conservation of the universe. There was goodness in God — goodness exceeding great. As yet it lay hidden in the heart of the Father, ready to be poured out at the proper time on the children of Adam and Eve.

Even then God was thinking thoughts of peace, of sending to us him who is our peace so that he might give us peace upon peace. His own loving kindness induced the Word of God enthroned on high to come down to us. His mercy drew him down, his fidelity to his promise to visit us kept him here and the spotless womb of the Virgin conceived him.

O Mother of God, O Sovereign Lady of the world, all generations shall call you blessed, because to all generations you have given life and glory. For in you the angels shall forever find gladness; the just, grace; and sinners, pardon. Rightly are the eyes of all the world directed toward you since it is in you and through you and from you that the kindly hand of the Almighty has renewed what he originally created.

Second Sermon for Pentecost, 2

As God comes to us, we need to go out to meet him.

Now we must earnestly search out the road by which he comes so that we may be able to go out to meet him as is fitting. However, as he came once on earth in visible flesh to work out our redemption so he comes daily in a hidden and spiritual way to save each individual soul. This spiritual coming of his is hidden: "Under his shadow we shall live among the nations." If the sick man is unable to go very far to meet such a great Physician, surely he should at least make an effort to lift his head and raise himself up a little to greet him as he approaches. It is not necessary for you to cross the seas, not necessary to pierce the clouds nor to climb the mountains to meet your God. It is not a lengthy order that is set before you. You have only to enter into yourself to find him. "For his word is very near you, it is on your lips and in your heart." Encounter him in compunction of heart and in confession of your sins so that you may at least leave behind you the dunghill of a defiled conscience, for the Author of purity could not be asked to enter such a place.
First Sermon of Advent, 10

In his enthusiasm, Bernard the novice pushed himself too hard and did lasting damage to his physical well-being. Twenty-five years later he would speak out strongly against this kind of rash fervor as he commented on the Song of Songs.

"Your name is oil poured out, therefore the maidens love you beyond measure." What does the bride mean by "beyond measure"? Greatly, vehemently, ardently. Shall I say that this spiritual doctrine may be indirectly applied to those of you who have recently arrived as a reproof of that indiscreet zeal or rather that incredibly obstinate intemperance which we have repeatedly attempted to restrain? You have no desire to be content with the common life. The regular fast is not enough for you nor the solemn vigils nor the rules of the house nor the amount of food and clothing we have allowed you. You want to have your own private ways rather than share what is common. In the beginning you entrusted yourselves to our care, why do you take charge of yourselves again? For now you have again for master not me but that self-will by which, on the testimony of your own consciences, you have so often offended God. It is that which urges you not to show pity for nature's needs, not to yield to reason, not to respect the advice or example of the seniors, not to obey us. Are you unaware that obedience is better than sacrifice? Have you not read in your Rule that what is done without permission of the spiritual father shall be ascribed to presumption and vainglory and not reckoned meritorious? Have you not read in the Gospel the example of obedience given by the boy Jesus as a way to holiness for young people? For when he had stayed behind in Jerusalem and explained that he must be busy about his Father's affairs, yet because his parents would not concur with him he did not disdain to follow them to Nazareth. So we have the Master obeying his disciples, God obeying humans, God's Word and Wisdom obeying a carpenter and his wife. And what is the comment of Sacred Scripture? It says, "He was subject to them." How long will you be wise in your own eyes? God entrusts himself to mortals and obeys them and will you still walk in your own ways?

On the Song of Songs, 19.7

Nonetheless, one must keep pressing forward. To stand still on this journey is to fall back.

Jacob in his vision saw angels ascending and descending the ladder but he did not see any standing still or sitting down. A fragile hanging ladder is no place for standing still nor, in the uncertain condition of this mortal life, can anyone remain unmovable in one position. We have not here an abiding city nor do we yet possess the one to come, we are still seeking it. Either we must go up or we must come down. We inevitably fall if we try to stand still. It is certain that the one who does not try to be better is not even good. When we stop trying to be better, then we cease to be good.

To the Assembly of Benedictine Abbots, Letter 91.2

Bernard warmly praised those who had the courage to press on to something better.

Your progress from good to better is no less wonderful, no less gratifying, than a conversion from evil to good. It is much easier to find those of the world who have been converted from evil to good than it is to find one religious who has progressed from good to better. Anyone who has risen even a little above the state he has once attained in religion is a very rare bird indeed. But your most salutary and remarkable action has not only given great joy to me, who wish so much to serve your holiness, but also to the whole Church, being all the more celebrated for being so rare.
To Abbot Richard of Fountains, Letter 96

On the other hand, Bernard has stern words for the one who has pressed forward to something better and then turned back. In this letter to a Benedictine abbot, Bernard gives evidence of his dependence on Pope St. Gregory the Great, something that marks his writings in general.

Facing page: *Moralia in Job* of St. Gregory. (Dijon Municipal Library)

Let everyone judge of himself as leniently as he likes, but I shall say what I think of myself. I, Bernard, if I had in will and deed passed freely from something good to something better, from something dangerous to something safer, and then afterwards willfully returned again to what I had left for the better, I would very much fear that I had rendered myself not only an apostate but also unfit for the Kingdom of God. And this is what blessed Gregory says, "Whoever attempts the best renders the second best unlawful for himself, since it is written, 'No one who puts his hand to the plough and then looks back is fit for the Kingdom of God.' Whoever has undertaken great things and then turns back to something less excellent is guilty of looking back."

To Geoffrey, Abbot of St. Mary's, York, Letter 313.5

Bernard would grow to be able to appreciate with more humor the life he embraced.

A good sort of playing this. . . . A good sort of playing which is ridiculous to human reason but a very beautiful sight to the angels. I say it is a good sort of playing by which we become an object of reproach to the rich and of ridicule to the proud. In fact what else do seculars think we are doing but playing when what they desire most on earth, we fly from and what they fly from, we desire? We are like acrobats and jugglers, heads down and feet in the air, standing or walking on their hands, drawing all eyes to themselves. But this is not a game for children or the theater where lust is excited by the effeminate and indecent contortions of the actors. It is a joyous game, decent, graceful and admirable, delighting the gaze of the heavenly onlookers. This pure and holy game he plays who says, "We have become a spectacle to angels and humans." And we, too, play this game that we may be ridiculed, discomforted, humbled until he comes who puts down the mighty from their seat and exalts the humble. May he gladden us and glorify us for ever.

To Canon Oger, Letter 87.12

In his talks to his monks and in his writings Bernard repeatedly traced out the spiritual journey and gave much practical advice to those who were walking on it drawing from his own lived experience. First one must turn from sin and the enticements of the world, the flesh, and the devil. . . .

You have such a victory over the temptations of the flesh that you no longer gratify its concupiscence nor yield to its enticements. This certainly is progress. You have surely gone forth from yourself. But you have not flown far unless by the purity of your mind you are able to rise above the images of sensible objects which are constantly rushing in upon you from every side. Until you have attained this, do not promise yourself any rest. You are in error if you think that the place of repose, the quiet of solitude, the perfection of light and the dwelling of peace can be found any nearer.

On the Song of Songs, 52.5

From curiosity...

Wherever they are, standing, walking, or sitting, their eyes are wandering, their glance darts right and left, their ears are cocked.... They used to watch over their own conduct, now all their watchfulness is for others.... My friend, if you gave yourself the attention you ought, I do not think you would have much time to look after others. Listen, busybody, to Solomon, listen to the words of the wise man for a fool, "Guard your heart with all care." Your senses will have quite enough to do to guard the source of life. You wander away from yourself. Whom have you left in charge?

The Steps of Humility and Pride, 28

From vaunting one's self...

When vanity has swelled the bladder to its limits a bigger vent must be made or the bladder will burst. As their silly merriment grows, laughing and signs are not enough outlet and they say like Elihu, "Behold, my heart is like new wine that has no vent; like new wineskins it is ready to burst." Yes, speak or burst! They are full of words and the swelling spirit strains within them. Their hunger and thirst are for listeners, someone to listen to their boasting, on whom they can pour out all their thoughts, someone they can show what big persons they are. At last the chance to speak comes. The discussion turns to literature. They bring forth from their treasury old things and new. They are not shy about producing their opinions; words are bubbling over. They do not wait to be asked. Their information comes before any questions. They ask questions, give the answers, cut off anyone who tries to speak. . . . They may have the capacity to help others but that is the least of their concerns. Their aim is not to teach you nor to be taught by you, but to show how much they know. If the conversation brings up the subject of religion, they are quite ready to talk of visions and dreams. They warmly recommend fasting, urge watching and exalt prayer above all. They will give a long discourse on patience and humility and

A Green Man (capital). Depicting the dangers of the "forbidden cup." Church of Saint-Pierre, Souvigny.

each of the other virtues — all words, all bragging. They trust that you will draw the conclusion, "Out of the abundance of the heart the mouth speaks." Or, "A good person from a good treasure brings forth good things."

The talk takes a lighter turn. They are more in their element here and become really eloquent. If you hear them, you will say their mouth has become a fountain of wit, a river of smart talk. They can set the most grave and serious laughing heartily. To say it briefly, when words are many, boasting is not lacking.
The Steps of Humility and Pride, 43

This journey with Christ is not a burdensome journey.

When I look for an example to illustrate this disburdening burden, nothing occurs to me more apt than the wings of a bird, for they, in an extraordinary way render the body both greater and yet more nimble. What a wonderful thing that a body should be made proportionately lighter by its very increase in size so that the more it increases in bulk the more it decreases in density. Here we have a clear illustration of the sweet burden of Christ which carries those who carry it.
To Rainald, Abbot of Foigny, Letter 72.2

Bernard saw clearly that not all pursue the journey in the same way.

All of us do not run with equal ardor.... Some are more eager for the study of wisdom, others concentrate on doing penance in the hope of pardon, others again are inspired to practice the virtues by the example of Christ's life and behavior, while yet others are roused to fervor more by the memory of his Passion.

Is it possible for us to find examples of each kind?

Those ran in the fragrance of wisdom who had been sent by the Pharisees and returned to them saying, "No man ever spoke like this man!" They admired his doctrine and praised his wisdom. Nicodemus also was lured into running by this fragrance when he came to Jesus by night, illumined by the light of his wisdom, and went back reformed, instructed in many things.

Mary Magdalene ran in the fragrance of justice. Many sins were forgiven her because she loved much....

The tax collector ran in similar fashion. Justice himself bears witness that after he had humbly implored forgiveness for his sins, he "went home again at rights with God."

Peter ran when, after his fall, he wept bitterly to wash away his sin and be restored to righteousness. David ran when he acknowledged and confessed his crime and was privileged to be told: "The Lord has put away your sin."

Paul testifies that he ran in the fragrance of holiness when he glories in being an imitator of Christ. He said to his followers: "Take me for a model as I take Christ."

And all those were running, too, who said: "We have left everything and followed you." It was because of the desire to follow Christ that they had left all things.

A general exhortation to everyone to follow in this fragrance is contained in the words: "Those who say they abide in Christ ought to walk in the same way in which he walked."

Finally, if you wish to hear of those who ran in the fragrance of the Passion, behold the martyrs.

On the Song of Songs, 22.9

Fundamental to Bernard's spiritual teaching is lectio divina, *that searching of Sacred Scripture to find Christ-God. Three different senses of Scripture are to be explored.*

By your leave then we shall search the Sacred Scripture for these three things, the garden, the storeroom, the bedroom. The one who thirsts for God eagerly studies and meditates on the inspired word. Know that there we are certain to find the one for whom we thirst. Let the garden, then, represent the plain, unadorned historical sense of Scripture, the storeroom its moral sense and the bedroom the mystery of divine contemplation.

For a start I feel my comparison of scriptural history to a garden is not unwarranted, for in it we find persons of many virtues like fruitful trees in the garden of the Bridegroom, in the Paradise of God. You may gather samples of their good deeds and good habits as you would apples from trees.

On the Song of Songs, 23.6-9

The consummation of our journey, union with God, is something we can know only by personal experience.

Grace alone can teach it, it cannot be learned except by experience. It is for the experienced, therefore, to recognize it and for others to burn with the desire, not so much of knowing as of feeling it, since this canticle is not a noise made by the mouth but a jubilation of heart, not a sound of the lips but a tumult of internal joys, not a symphony of voices but a harmony of wills. It is not heard outside, for it does not sound externally. The singer alone can hear it and he to whom it is sung, namely the bridegroom and the bride. For it is a nuptial song, celebrating the chaste and joyous embraces of loving hearts, the concord of minds and the union resulting from reciprocal affection.
On the Song of Songs, 1.11

This union with God is an experience we can seek and enjoy repeatedly.

If we fervently persist with prayers and tears, the Bridegroom will return each time and not defraud us of our express desires. But only to disappear soon again and not to return again unless he is sought for with all our heart. And so, even in this body we can often enjoy the happiness of the Bridegroom's presence but it is a happiness that is never complete because the joy of his visit is followed by the pain of his departure. The beloved has no choice but to endure this state until the hour when we lay down the body's weary weight and raised aloft by the wings of desire freely traverse the meadows of contemplation and in spirit follow the One we love without restraint wherever he goes.

On the Song of Songs, 32.2

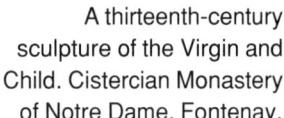

A thirteenth-century sculpture of the Virgin and Child. Cistercian Monastery of Notre Dame, Fontenay.

Bernard gives the witness of his own experience.

But let me tell you what I have attained to or rather what I believe myself to have attained to. And you must not regard as a boast this communication which I make only for your own good.... There is a place where the Lord appears truly tranquil and at rest. It is the place neither of the judge nor of the teacher but of the bridegroom. It becomes for me (whether for others also, I do not know) a real bedchamber whenever it is granted me to enter there.... If, my brothers, it should ever be granted to you to be so transported for a time into this secret sanctuary of God and there be so rapt and absorbed as to be distracted or disturbed by no necessity of the body, no importunity or care, no stinging of conscience or, what is more difficult to avoid, no inrush of corporal images from the sense of imagination, you can truly say, "The King has brought me into his bedchamber."

On the Song of Songs, 23.11-16

You ask then how I know he was present when his ways can in no way be traced? He is life and power and as soon as he enters in, he awakens my slumbering soul. He stirs and soothes and pierces my heart, for before it was hard as stone and diseased. So he has begun to pluck out and destroy, to build up and to plant, to water dry places and illumine dark ones, to open what was closed and to warm what was cold, so that my soul may bless the Lord and all that is within me may praise his holy name.

So when the Word came to me, he never made known his coming by any signs: not by sight, not by sound, not by touch. It was not by any movement of his that I perceived his coming. Only by the movement of my heart did I perceive his presence. I knew the power of his might because my faults were put to flight and my human yearnings brought into subjection. But when he has left me, all these spiritual powers become weak and faint and begin to grow cold. As often as he slips away from me, so often shall I call him back. As long as I live, the word "return," for the recall of the Word, will be on my lips.

On the Song of Songs 74.6f

Bernard is very conscious of public opinion; in many of his letters, he relates to issues regarding his own self-image and the criticisms of others.

To his most beloved Lord, Abbot Hugh, all that he could wish for himself, from Brother Bernard of Clairvaux.

As far as I can gather from your letter it appears that either I have worded myself less clearly than I had wished or else that you have not understood me in the way I had intended you to do. The warning I gave you of the consequences of receiving that monk was quite genuine. I really did fear then and I still do, as I wrote to you. But I had no intention of trying to persuade you or advise you, still less did I mean, as you said I did, that the monk ought to be returned to his monastery. As I have known his wish to join us for a long time, I ought rather to have congratulated him than urge his return. But when I was implored by his abbot, with whom I am very intimate, and by the Archbishop of Reims, to write to you and ask for his return, I tried so far as I could both to clear myself of any suspicion of complicity in the affair and to warn you of the abuse you might incur by your action, while at the same time satisfying them. Knowing your shrewdness I thought you would read between the lines and see this. Or that at any rate you would gather what I meant from what I put at the end of the letter, if you read it in the spirit in which it was written. For when I had warned you of the consequences which I feared, and not without cause, might come of your receiving this monk, I added, if I remember right, "Should you prefer to endure all this rather than lose the man, that is your affair and you must see to it." These, or very nearly these, were my words. I had intended by saying this at the end of the letter to give you a covert hint that I had written what I did under pressure to satisfy, not to say hood-wink, others.

What you say about my insinuating to this monk by means of the messenger that if he came to me I would obtain secretly a dispensation from Rome is, I assure you by the very Truth, quite untrue. Is it likely that I would boast or even hope that I could receive a monk from a monastery which is well-known to me, whom I do not think even you can keep without grave offence? But even were this so, even if I did envy you the monk and try to attract him to myself, hoping or pretending I could engineer his dispensation from Rome, is it likely that I would reveal to the messenger of all people that I was plotting against his own monastery? I must tell you, so that you may not think the affection you have had for me hitherto has been misplaced, that I shall consider it my duty to continue to work for your interests as I see them, as hard as I do for my own or even harder, and this not so that the harmony between us may be further strengthened,

as I have done hitherto, but that it may not now be altogether broken. What more can I say? Only that I could never have believed you capable of such an action as you, on the sole ground of mere suspicion, attribute to me.
   To Abbot Hugh of Pontigny, Letter 33

The thirteenth-century façade of the Cistercian Abbey of Notre Dame in Pontigny, France.

For Bernard, as famous as he was for his style and rhetoric, writing was both a journey and a responsibility. One can relate to him as a pilgrim on the road trying to express himself as precisely as possible. In the following letter, he comments about the labor of writing.

And where, I ask you, is the leisure, where the quiet of silence when one is thinking, composing and writing? You say that all this can be done in silence. I am surprised that you can seriously mean this. How can the mind be quiet when composing a letter and a turmoil of expressions are clamoring and every sort of phrase and diversity of senses are jostling one another; when words spring into the mind but just the word one wants escapes one; when literary effect, sense and how to convey a meaning clearly and what should be said and in what order it should be said have to be carefully considered — all the things which those who understand these matters scrutinize carefully? Do you tell me there is any quiet in all this? Can you call this silence, even if the lips are not moving?

To Canon Oger, Letter 88.1

It is very difficult to be a lonely pilgrim on the road to the heavenly Jerusalem. Indeed, Bernard had his brother monks in Clairvaux as his primary support group. Yet, among his very complex relations in the outside world, he had other friends with whom he communicated and from whom he received a lot of feedback, support, and encouragement. His letters mirror both his attitudes concerning friendship as well as his friendly relations with these individuals.

No one knows what is in us save our own human spirit that is within us. We see only on the surface, God alone can search the heart. Yet you have been able to weigh and mutually to compare our affection for each other so as to deliver a verdict not only on the state of your own heart but even on that of another. I wonder how or on what grounds you have been able to do this and I cannot wonder enough. It is an error to which the human mind is ever prone not only to consider good to be evil, what is true to be false and what is false to be true but also to be doubtful about what is certain and certain about what is doubtful. You may be right when you say that my affection for you is less than yours is for me but I am certainly certain that you cannot be certain. How can you know for certain what it is certain you cannot be certain about? . . . But wonderful to say, you have been able to assert, with I know not what grounds for your confidence, "My affection for you is greater than yours is for me.". . .

Because your charity is greater than mine, that is all the more reason why you should not despise my smaller capacity because, although you love more than I do, you do not love more than you are able. And I, too, although I love you less than I should, yet I love you as much as I can according to the power that has been given me. Draw me after you that I may reach you and with you receive more fully from whence comes the power to love.

Why do you try to reach me and complain that you are not able? You could reach me if you but considered what I am and you can reach me still whenever you wish, if you are content to find me as I am and not as you wish me to be. I cannot think what else you see in me besides what I am, what it is you are chasing which is not me. You do not overtake it because it is not me, because I am not able to be what you would like me to be. To use your own words, I do not fail you, it is God in me who fails you.

And now if all this trifling pleases you, tell me and I will give you more. . . .

To William, Abbot of St. Thierry, Letter 85

To another friend Bernard writes:

I have answered your short letters with short letters, glad to have an excuse in your brevity for being brief myself. It is true, as you rightly say, eternal friendships are not helped by exchanging vain and empty words. However much you try to show your friendship by verses, phrases and quotations, I feel sure you express less than you feel. And you would not be wrong if you believed the same thing of me. When your letter was delivered into my hands, you were already in my heart. While I write this letter you are present to me, as I am sure I shall be present to you when you read it. We wear ourselves out scribbling to each other and we exhaust our messengers in sending them backwards and forwards between us. But is the spirit ever weary of loving? Let us stop this tiring business of exchanging letters and turn ourselves to what the more we do the easier it becomes. Let us give our heads a respite from dictating, our tongues from chattering, our hands from writing, our messengers from running to and fro and apply ourselves to meditating day and night on the law of the Lord, which is the law of charity. The more we rest from doing this, the less rested we become. The more we apply ourselves to it, the more repose we derive from it. Let us love and be loved, benefitting ourselves

St. Bernard became a source of constant inspiration for monks all over Europe. This sculpture of St. Bernard stands in La Poblet, Spain.

by loving and others by being loved. We find rest in those we love and we provide a resting place for those who love us. To love anyone in God is charity, to try to make ourselves loved for God's sake is the service of charity.

To Canon Oger, Letter 90.1

Another friend to whom Bernard of Clairvaux frequently addressed letters was Bernard the Carthusian, who was later called forth from the Charterhouse of Portes-en-Bugey to be Bishop of Belley. We have here also one of many examples of how Bernard depended on his friends to help evaluate his literary work.

My dearest Bernard, I cannot hide my sorrow nor can I disguise from you any longer the grief which I suffer. I have not forgotten my long-standing promise to you. I have for long had the firm intention and great desire to pass by you, so that I may see again those whom my soul loves and, in their company, find consolation for my journey, relief for my labors and healing for my sins. But in punishment for my sins it has come about that regretfully I find that I am not able to do so. I acknowledge this not as a fault but as a punishment for my faults. I beg you to understand, man of God, that it is not at all that I do not care for my friends nor is it that I am lazy or negligent in the matter but simply that I am prevented by the work of God which I cannot ignore. My vexation gnaws at me like a worm and my grief is ever with me. I am troubled enough on other accounts but, I must confess, on none so much as on this. It vexes me more than all the labors of my journey, than the discomfort of the heat, than the anxiety of my responsibilities. Now that I have exposed my wound to my friend, it is your business to have pity on me and relieve me by sharing my burden. I implore your prayers and the prayers of the holy men with whom you live. I am sending you the sermons on the beginning of the Song of Solomon as you have asked me to do and as I have promised. When you have read them, I beg you to write as soon as you conveniently can and tell me whether you think I should continue with them or not.

Letter 154

◆

One of Bernard's greatest sorrows was the betrayal he suffered at the hands of his most trusted secretary, Nicholas. He first speaks of it in this letter to Pope Eugene, not yet suspecting the betrayer is so close at hand.

I am in danger from false brethren. Many forged letters have gone out under a forgery of my seal. And, what I fear may have happened, these forgeries are said to have reached even you. This is why I have rejected my old seal and am, as you see, using a new one for the future, containing both my image and name. Do not any longer accept the other seal as coming from me, except in the case of the Bishop of Clermont to whom I gave a letter with that seal before I had this one made.

Letter 284

Demonic Spirits (capital). Souvigny, twelfth century.

When the matter came fully to light, Bernard wrote to the Pope with a certain bitterness.

Nicholas has left because he was not one of us. He has gone leaving behind him foul traces. I knew for sometime what sort of man he was but I was waiting either for God to convert him or for him to betray himself like Judas. And this is what has happened. When he left there was found on his person, besides books, money and much gold, three seals, one his own, the other the prior's and the third mine, not the old one but the new one which I was obliged to have made on account of his cunning and frauds. I remember having written to you about this without mentioning any names, saying merely that I was in danger from false brethren. Who can tell to how many people he has written saying anything he wanted under my seal but without my knowledge. I sincerely hope that your Curia may be cleansed of his filthy lies and that the very innocence of those who are with me may serve to excuse them to those who have been deceived and baffled by his lying. It has been partly proved and he has partly admitted that he has written to you falsely not once but several times. His foul deeds have poisoned my lips or your ears by mentioning them. He boasts that he has friends in the Curia so if he comes to you remember Arnold of Bres-

cia [who stirred up in Rome revolt against the Pope] because a worse than he is here. No one has better deserved life imprisonment, no one deserves more a sentence of perpetual silence.
To Pope Eugene III, Letter 298

Bernard was not unaware of the many gifts he had received from God and of the importance of rendering due thanks to the Giver.

I know that there are some people who are, as it were, wisely ignorant of the gifts they have received from the Lord for fear that they may become puffed up with pride and fall into the snare of the devil if they pay attention to them. But for myself I think it is a good thing to know what I have received from the Lord so that I may also know what I lack. With the Apostle, I think it my duty to recognize what God has bestowed upon me so that I may know what to pray and sigh for. A person who has received a gift and yet does not know what sort of gift it is stands in the twofold danger of being both ungrateful for what he has received and careless in guarding it. . . . May the Lord save me from the disgraceful ingratitude of that people about whom it was said, "They had forgotten all his mercies, all those wonderful deeds of his they had witnessed." Even those of the world hold that no one should ever forget a kindness. It is therefore important that we should know how to guard what we have received and that the grace of God should not be without fruit in our lives. So that his grace may abide always with us, we should never cease to give thanks for it to the Lord our God.

To Bishop Peter of Palencia, Letter 372

Bernard's affections did not limit themselves to those of his own gender. He addressed warm letters of affection to women as well, cherishing his relationships with them. To one generous countess, Ermengarde, who had become a nun, he wrote:

To his beloved daughter in Christ, once a distinguished countess, but now a humble handmaid of Christ, the respectful affection of a holy love from Bernard, Abbot of Clairvaux.

I wish I could find words to express what I feel toward you! If you could but read in my heart how great an affection for you the finger of God has there inscribed then you would surely see how no tongue could express and no pen describe what the spirit of God has been able to inscribe there. Absent from you in body, I am always present to you in spirit and, although neither of us can come to the other, you have it within your power not yet indeed to know me, but at any rate to guess something of what I feel. Do not ever suppose that your affection for me is greater than mine for you and so believe yourself superior to me inasmuch as you think your love surpasses mine. Search your heart and you will find mine there, too, and ascribe to me at least as great an affection for you as you find there for me. But your modesty is so great that you are more likely to believe that he who has moved you to esteem me and choose me as your spiritual counsellor has also moved me with a like feeling of affectionate concern for you. It is for you to see that you have me always by you. For my part, I confess, I am never without you and never leave you. I wanted to scribble these few brief lines to you from the road while traveling. And I hope, if God wills, to write to you more fully when I have the leisure.

To Ermengarde, Letter 116

Like any other human being Bernard knew his moments of discouragement. The failure of the Second Crusade, the responsibility for which some laid at Bernard's door, brought on such a moment for him. At such a time he was able to unburden himself with friends.

It is only right you should know how things are going with me. I have decided to stay in my monastery and not go out, except once a year for the general chapter of abbots at Cîteaux. Here, supported by your prayers and consoled by your good will, I shall remain for the few days that are left to me in which to fight until the time comes for me to be relieved at my post. May God be merciful and never alienate his mercy or your prayers from me. I am broken in body and have a legitimate excuse for not going about as I used to do. I shall stay and hold my peace so that perhaps I may experience something of that inner sweetness of which the Prophet sings, "If deliverance you would have from the Lord, in silence await it." And, so as not to appear the only one to make fun of me, I suppose you will not now dare to reproach me with my silence and in no way call it sloth. . . . Commend me to the prayers of your holy brethren at Cluny having first, if you think fit, greeted them from me as the servant of them all.
To Peter the Venerable, Letter 228

For Bernard the source, the center, and the consummation of this whole journey remains ever the Lord Jesus Christ.

What have you to do with righteousness if you are ignorant of Christ, who is the righteousness of God? Where, I ask, is true prudence, except in the teaching of Christ? Or true justice, if not from Christ's mercy? Or true temperance, if not in Christ's life? Or true fortitude, if not in Christ's Passion? Only those can be called prudent who are imbued with his teaching. Only those are just who have had their sins pardoned through his mercy. Only those are temperate who take pains to follow his way of life. Only those are courageous who hold fast to the example of his patience when buffeted by sufferings. Vainly therefore will anyone strive to acquire the virtues if he thinks they may be obtained from any source other than the Lord of virtues whose teaching is the seed-bed of prudence, whose mercy is the wellspring of justice, whose life is a mirror of temperance, whose death is the badge of fortitude.

On the Song of Songs, 22.11

Our guide and support on the journey is this our God who has come into this world.

Our Savior is a faithful counsellor who can never deceive us or be deceived. He is a strong helper whom labor never wearies. He is a mighty protector who will quickly enable us to trample underfoot the powers of Satan. For he is the wisdom of God who is ever ready to instruct the ignorant, the power of God for whom it is so easy to strengthen the weak and rescue those in danger. Therefore, my brothers and sisters, in all our doubts and perplexities let us have recourse to so wise a Master. In all our undertakings let us invoke the assistance of so powerful a helper. In our every combat let us commit our souls to the keeping of so faithful a protector. He has come into the world for this purpose, that living here in us with us and for us, he might illumine our darkness, lighten our labors and guard us from all dangers.

Seventh Sermon for Advent, 2

In Jesus' sweet name we find all.

Do we feel sad? Let the name of Jesus come into our heart, from there let it spring to our mouth, so that shining like the dawn it may dispel all darkness and make a cloudless sky. Do we fall into sin? Does despair even urge us to suicide? Let us but invoke this life-giving name and our will to live will be at once renewed. The hardness of heart that is our common experience, the apathy bred of indolence, bitterness of mind, repugnance for the things of the spirit — have they ever failed to yield in the presence of that saving name? The tears dammed up by the barrier of our pride — how have they not burst forth again with sweeter abundance at the thought of Jesus' name? And where is the one who, terrified and trembling before impending peril, has not been suddenly filled with courage and rid of fear by calling on the strength of the name? Where is the one who, tossed on the rolling waves of doubt, did not quickly find certitude by recourse to the clarity of Jesus' name? Was ever a person so discouraged, so beaten down by affliction, to whom the sound of this name did not bring new resolve? In short, for all the ills and disorders to which flesh is heir this name is medicine. For proof we have no less than his own promise, "Call upon me in the day of trouble. I will deliver you, and you

shall glorify me." Nothing so curbs the onset of anger, so allays the upsurge of pride. It cures the wound of envy, controls unbridled extravagances and quashes the flame of lust. It cools the thirst of covetousness and banishes the itch of unclean desire. For when I name Jesus I set before me a man who is meek and humble of heart, kind, prudent, chaste, merciful, flawlessly upright and holy in the eyes of all. And this same man is the all-powerful God whose way of life heals me, whose support is my strength. All these re-echo for me at the hearing of Jesus' name.
On the Song of Songs, 15.6

As we look through the exceptionally large collection of letters that has come down to us from St. Bernard, we are amazed at the breadth of his concerns and of his contacts. His influence with people in high station is very evident. He writes countless letters on behalf of bishops and archbishops from all parts of Christendom — Reims, Canterbury, Mainz, London, Troyes, Salamanca, Cambrai, Auxerre, Arras, Angers, Orléans, Le Mans, and Beauvais, and also on behalf of cardinals and kings and such outstanding figures as Suger (Abbot of St. Denis), Peter the Venerable (Abbot of Cluny), and the Prior of the Grand Chartreuse. He was in his advocacy at times a bit naïve, taken in by his own enthusiasm and others' shrewdness.

You know I have stood up for the king to my Lord the Pope, how absent in body yet present in spirit I spoke out on his behalf. Indeed the king made fair promises. But now he is returning evil for good and I am obliged to write in a contrary vein. I am ashamed of the mistake I made about him and of the false hopes I cherished of him and I am very glad that I was not listened to when, in my simplicity, I spoke for him. I thought to serve a peace-loving king and I find that I have helped a bitter antagonist of the Church.

To Stephen, Cistercian Cardinal Bishop of Palestrina, Letter 224

On another occasion he wrote a terse note to Pope Eugene III in none-too-gentle language.

A serpent has deceived me! A double-faced cunning wretch, void of all righteousness, afraid of an interview, an enemy of his own conscience, set on the injury of the brethren, has without my knowledge obtained letters of recommendation from me through the Bishop of Beauvais. (For what would I not do for this man?) If you do not wish my conscience to be even further burdened, see that this cunning villain gains nothing and is not able to use any letter of mine for persecuting innocent people. Although even this would not satisfy me if this evil swindler and greedy extortioner were not made to pay the penalty of his misdeeds.

Letter 269

There was a certain cleverness about Bernard, call it diplomacy if you will, in the way he could set forth a petition or in his turn deny one. Thus he writes to the Count of Champagne on whom he depended for so much patronage.

You know that I care for you, but how much I do so, God knows better than you. I am quite sure that you, too, are fond of me but for the sake of God. Therefore if I should offend God, you would have no reason for your affection since then God would not be with me. Why should a great prince like you care for an insignificant creature like me unless you believed that God were with me? So perhaps it would not be to your advantage for me to offend God. But I would certainly offend God were I to do what you want me to do.
To Count Theobald, Letter 271

Bernard, of course, depended in good part upon secretaries to aid him. But he was not always well served by them. In a letter to Peter the Venerable he speaks of both of the help and of the deficiency of it.

To his most reverend Father and dear Friend, Peter, by the grace of God Abbot of Cluny, health and greetings in the source of all true health, from Brother Bernard, Abbot of Clairvaux.

Would that I were able to express in this letter all that I feel toward you! Then you would certainly see clearly the love for you which God has inscribed upon my heart and engraved upon my very bones.... I say this because my son Nicholas [one of Bernard's secretaries], who is your son also, is himself greatly disturbed and has greatly disturbed me by telling me that he noticed that one of my letters to you concluded with bitter words. Believe me who love you that nothing could have come from my heart or left my lips which would have offended your ears. My many occupations are to blame because when my secretaries have not fully grasped my meaning they are apt to write too sharply and I do not have time to read through what they have written. Forgive me this time, for whatever I may do with other letters I shall in the future look through my letters to you and trust in no one's ears or eyes but my own. The rest will be more

fully and more clearly recounted to you by our common son. Harken to him as you would to myself who love you so dearly, not in mere words, but in deed and truth. Greet for me all your holy brethren and pray them to pray for me.
Letter 387

A man as strong and forthright in his expression as Bernard could hardly help offending others, yet he knew how to humble himself and seek to make amends.

I want you to know I do not regard it as a small matter to have offended you in any way. On the contrary it is causing me much sorrow. I call upon God to witness that in my imagination I come to you as a suppliant as I cannot come in body. I see myself before you making humble satisfaction on bended knees. Would that the Holy Spirit who perhaps inspires me to do this would make you feel how sadly and unhappily I throw myself in spirit at your knees. How often with naked shoulders and scourge ready in my hands, prepared as if at your command to punish myself, I implore your forgiveness and anxiously await your pardon. If it is no trouble to you I beg you to let me know as soon as you can whether you have forgiven me so that if you are satisfied I can feel confident of your pardon. If not, I can humble myself yet more and demand something yet more of myself, if I can, so as to make worthy amends.

To Abbot Alvius of Anchin, Letter 65

Bernard also knew how to use others to help him in this task of reconciliation.

I beg that you may be so good as to forward the enclosed letter to the Abbot of Anchin and that, when an opportunity presents itself, you will do what you can for an absent friend in the matter with which the letter is concerned. For whether it be just or unjust I ought not to ignore resentment against me, especially when it is on the part of such a father as the Abbot of Anchin. I could have better appeased his anger by word of mouth than by letter, for, in matters like this, the living word is better than the written word and the tongue than the pen. The pen cannot so well express the sincerity of the speaker. And so because I cannot go to him in person to apologize, I am trying to do what I can through you. I beg you again and again to do what you can to remove this offence from the Kingdom of God which is within us.

To Abbot Geoffrey of St. Medard, Letter 66

While Bernard was well known for his spirit of recollection he nonetheless was not failing in his power of observation. His writings are full of indications of this as in this passage from his sermons on the Song of Songs where he shows that he did not overlook feminine charm.

"Your cheeks are beautiful as the turtle dove's." The bride's modesty is a delicate thing; flush suffused her face, so heightening her beauty . . . this blood that spreads evenly beneath the surface of her pearly skin, quietly mingling with it to enhance her physical beauty by the pink and white loveliness of her cheeks.
On the Song of Songs, 40.1

Enlightened man of God though he be, Bernard shared in the sexist prejudices of the prevailing patriarchy. They come out in this letter to a reigning queen.

To the most illustrious Queen of Jerusalem, Melisande, that she may find favor with the Lord, from Bernard, Abbot of Clairvaux.

Receive a brief but useful word of advice from a distant land, as a small seed which will bear a great harvest in time. Receive advice from a friend who is seeking your honor and not his own ends. No one can give you more loyal advice than one who loves you and not your possessions. The king, your husband, being dead, and the young king still unfit to discharge the affairs of a kingdom and fulfill the duty of a king, the eyes of all will be upon you and on you alone the whole burden of the kingdom will rest. You must set your hand to great things and, although a woman, you must act as a man by doing all you have to in a spirit prudent and strong. You must arrange all things prudently and discreetly so that all may judge you from your actions to be a king rather than a queen and so that the Gentiles may have no occasion for saying, "Where is the king of Jerusalem?" But you will say, "Such things are beyond my power, they are great matters which far exceed my strength and my knowledge. They are the duties of a man and I am only a woman, weak in body, changeable of heart, not far-seeking in counsel nor accustomed to business." I know, my daughter, I know that these are great matters but I also know that although the raging of the sea is great, the Lord is great in heaven. These are great affairs, but great, too, is our Lord and great his power.

Letter 354

Bernard also held to contemporary ideas about medicine, which might have been well justified given the relatively primitive state of the medical art.

To his very dear sons in Christ, the Brethren of St. Anastasius, greetings and prayers from Brother Bernard, Abbot of Clairvaux.

There is one thing your venerable abbot [Bernard Paganelli, who was to become Pope Eugene III] has asked me about which does not seem to me at all good. And I believe that I have the Spirit of God and know the will of God in the matter. I fully realize that you live in an unhealthy region [the monastery was in the Campagna, just outside of Rome, an area infested with malaria] and that many of you are sick. But remember him who said, "I delight to boast of the weaknesses that humiliate me so that the strength of Christ may enshrine itself in me" and "When I am weak then I am strongest of all." I have the very greatest sympathy for bodily sickness, but I consider that sickness of the soul is much more to be feared and avoided. It is not at all in keeping with our profession to seek bodily medicines and they are not really conducive to health. The use of common herbs, such as are used by the poor, can sometimes be tolerated and such is our custom. But to buy special kinds of medicines, to seek out doctors and swallow their prescriptions, this does not become religious, is contrary to simplicity and is especially inconsistent with the decency and simplicity of our Order. We know that those who live according to the merely natural cannot be acceptable to God. For us who have received no spirit of worldly wisdom but the spirit that comes from God the proper medicine is humility and the most suitable prayer is, "Purge me of my sin, the guilt which I freely acknowledge." This is the health you must try to obtain, seek out and preserve, dearest brothers, because vain is the help of human persons.

Letter 345

Bernard's gifts in the field of music and liturgy were perhaps surer, though not all would agree on this. In any case he had very definite ideas that he did not hesitate to set forth.

To Guy, the venerable Abbot of Montieramey, and the holy brothers who are with him, from Bernard, their servant, that they might serve the Lord in holiness.

Men should not fail to praise One who has been glorified by the angels, but in their celebrations anything savoring of novelty or frivolity would be out of place. There is room here only for the authentic and the traditional which edifies the Church and bears the stamp of her dignity. If something new is to be heard, because the situation requires it, I believe, as I have said, those things are to be used which will please the hearts of the hearers and be useful to them because of the dignity both of the expression and of the author. Furthermore, the texts must be clear, shining forth with unclouded truth, proclaiming justice, urging humility, teaching equity. They should bring forth truth in our mind, virtue in our actions; crucify our vices, inflame devotion and discipline our senses. The chant if it is employed should be quite solemn, nothing sensuous or rustic. Its sweetness should not be frivolous. It should please the ear only that it might move the heart, taking away sorrow and

mitigating wrath. It should not detract from the sense of the words but rather make it more fruitful. It is not a little blow to spirituality when more attention is paid to feats of voice than to the meaning of the words.
Letter 398

◆ FOUR

A Voice at the Crossroads for the Church

In 1073 the former Abbot of St. Paul-Outside-the-Walls (of Rome) was elected Pope. Hildebrand took the name Gregory VII and energetically launched a reform not only to free the Church from secular domination but to assert the superiority of the spiritual power over the temporal and to call the members of the Church, especially the clergy, to a moral renewal. At his death in 1085 much of his agenda remained yet to be achieved. It was the principles of the Gregorian reform that totally informed the activity of the Abbot of Clairvaux.

Bernard had gone apart to be free from the cares and concerns of the world. Yet he could not enter into a deep union with Christ without being taken up with his Beloved's cares and concerns, above all with care for Christ's Body, the Church. "God's affairs are my affairs; nothing that concerns him is foreign to me." The role of the

Cloister of St. Paul-Outside-the-Walls in Rome.

Pope as the head of that Body on earth not only called forth Bernard's loyalty and obedience; when it became uncertain as to who was called to fulfill that role, Bernard was filled with solicitude. The Church was at a crossroads and the way was uncertain. Louis VI, King of France, called upon Bernard to discern who was the true Pope. After prayer, the man of God had no doubt. With a commanding sureness he pointed to Innocent. He then went on to win over to Innocent II the support of the King of Germany (later Holy Roman Emperor), Lothair; the King of England, Henry I; and many others until in 1138 he finally obtained the submission of the antipope himself.

Through the years Bernard repeatedly refused the miter: Milan, Langres, Reims. . . . He nonetheless intervened in many episcopal elections. Wherever a challenge came to his attention, with a sureness that is a bit frightening, the saint used his influence at Rome and elsewhere to seat the man whom he thought would best promote the Gregorian principles of a bishopric independent of the secular authority and closely united to a Supreme Pontiff.

The internal unity and moral uprightness that he sought for the Church had to be based on sound doctrine. When such orthodoxy seemed to be threatened, men looked to Bernard to bring all the authority of his pen and presence to its defense. Heretics, one after the other — Arnold of Brescia, Peter of Bruys, Gilbert of Porree — experienced his chastening power.

A new more rational approach to theology had begun among monks over a century earlier. It flourished in the city and cathedral schools. It reached a sparkling ascendancy in the happenstance monk, Peter Abelard. This brilliant man's keen mind carried faith's search for reason farther than any of his predecessors. Fallible reason began to prevail over faith. The Church was at another crossroads.

Bernard, the last of the Fathers of the Church and equal to the first of them, was called upon to speak out. Friendship (both his love for William of St. Thierry who repeatedly implored him to intervene and for Peter Abelard whom Bernard saw as being in danger of losing his soul) and his zeal for the Church and for the Truth — who Bernard saw as Christ his Beloved — fired his mighty rhetoric. Bernard rendered Abelard to silence and hounded him into a cloistered exile. (He fired off at least ten letters to Rome, besides helping others to write, to gain a preemptive condemnation.) But the seeds of scholasticism were well planted and the trend of the hour would prevail and ultimately flourish. However, history may yet be vindicating the voice at the crossroads.

Was not the theological reaction of the Reformation more in the spirit of Bernard and responding to the same excesses that he saw in Peter Abelard? More recently, is not the theological renewal of this century, given such powerful impetus by the Second Vatican Council, reaching back over the long scholastic parenthesis that has dominated the Catholic theological community since it reacted to the Reformation and taking up again the rich patristic

St. Silvester riding into Rome. A twelfth-century mural mosaic in the Chapel of St. Silvester in the Monastery of the Four Crowns, Rome.

heritage that Bernard of Clairvaux crowned in the twelfth century?

Bernard's own crowning hour seemed to come on February 15, 1145, when the cardinals without dispute elected his spiritual son and disciple to the See of Peter. Bernard Paganelli, Abbot of Tre Fontane, took the name Eugene III. Bernard himself would write to the Pope: "People say you are not the pope and that I am. Those with business for the papal court come to me from all sides...." His influence was great. He wrote five books entitled *On Consideration* to guide the Pope in his conduct and way of life, books that have continued to guide popes down through the centuries. Yet he who was father knew also how to be an obedient son. He not only preached the principles of the Gregorian reform and sought to get others to adopt them, he personally lived them. His obedience to his son-pope was to make enormous demands on his waning strength and lead him into his darkest hour.

Even though he withdrew into a monastery and did not seek ecclesiastical preferment, Bernard of Clairvaux had a great love for the Church, the Lord's own vineyard. It was often the subject of his preaching, especially when he wrote his very popular commentary on the Song of Songs.

If we follow the text's direct meaning, satisfied with what words mean as they stand, we shall imagine we are reading in our holy Scripture about those material and earthly vineyards that draw daily nourishment from the dew of heaven and the fertile soil, whence they produce the wine that ministers to wantonness. But by doing this we shall have deduced from writings so holy and divine nothing worthy.... Is it for vineyards that God is concerned? But if, in a spiritual sense, we understand the vineyards to be the churches, to be the peoples who are believers, as the Prophet did when he said: "The vineyard of the Lord of hosts is the house of Israel," ... note in a special way how the Church extended her boundaries into vineyards of this kind all over the world from that day on which she was attacked by her mother's sons in Jerusalem and banished from it along with her first new plantation — that company of believers who were described as "of one heart and soul."

It did not perish, it changed to a new location. It even increased and spread further afield under the blessing of the Lord. So lift up your eyes round about and see if the mountains were not covered with its shade, the cedars of God with its branches, if its tendrils did not extend to the sea and its offshoots all the way to the river. Don't be surprised by this; it is God's building, God's farm. He waters it, he propagates it, prunes and cleanses it that it may bear more fruit. When did he ever deprive of his care and labor that which his right hand planted? There can be no question of neglect where the apostles are the branches, the Lord is the vine and his Father the vinedresser. Planted in faith, its roots are grounded in love, dug in with the hoe of discipline, fertilized with penitential tears and watered with the words of preachers. So it abounds with the wine that inspires joy rather than debauchery, wine full of the pleasure that is never licentious. This is the wine that gladdens our hearts, the wine that even the angels drink with gladness. From one vineyard that seemed to have been destroyed by the storm of savage persecution, what a vast number have been propagated and flourish all over the world!

On the Song of Songs, 30.2-4

The vineyard is one of the most recurring themes in Bernard's writings. This vineyard was photographed at harvesttime in the Land of the Bible.

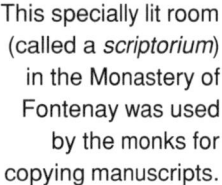

This specially lit room (called a *scriptorium*) in the Monastery of Fontenay was used by the monks for copying manuscripts.

In the years he was championing the disputed papacy of Innocent II, letters flowed to the Pontiff in a steady stream. He was conscious of their frequency.

I am always writing to you. Every day brings you my letters and petitions. I am torn in two ways. On the one hand I do not want to fail my friends and on the other I am loath to trouble you. Affection spurs me on, diffidence holds me back and shame almost prevents me from fulfilling the demands of charity. The bride of Christ has nowhere to lay her head, no refuge in time of trouble save with the friend of the Bridegroom.

Letter 351

In fact, Innocent did not long survive, dying on September 24, 1143. His two successors enjoyed very short reigns: Celestine II less than six months and Lucius II less than a year. Bernard was then able to welcome to the throne his spiritual son, Bernard Paganelli, the Abbot of Tre Fontane, and begin again his powerful intercessory role. In his first letter to the new Pope we can hear a whole array of emotions and sentiments: a certain hurt that the Pope had not personally written to inform him of the election, a struggle to come to terms with the new roles, a sure sense that his word will still carry weight with the new Pontiff and a righteousness that again brings forward the affair of York.

The glad tidings of what the Lord has done for you has been heard in our land and is on everybody's lips. I have not written sooner because I have been thinking it over in silence. I was waiting to hear from you, "to be met on the way with abundant blessings." I was waiting for a trusty messenger from your person to tell me everything exactly as it all happened. I was waiting to see if perhaps one of my sons would not come back to soothe the grief of his father and say: "Your son Jacob still lives, and it is he that rules the whole land of Egypt." So I am writing not of my own free will but of necessity, constrained thereto by friends to whom I cannot deny whatever little remains to me of my life. (Few are the days left to me, now there only remains the grave.)

Now that I have begun, I will not keep silence but will speak to my Lord. I do not dare to call you a son any longer. You were my son, but now you have become my father. I was your father, but now I have become your son. You who came after me, have been preferred before me. But I am not jealous, for I am sure that you who not only came after me but also, in a manner, through me will make up in your person for what is lacking to me. For, if you will pardon my saying so, it was I who as it were begot you in the Gospel. What is it that I hope will be my joy and a glorious crown for me? It is you before God. A wise son is the pride of his father. . . .

But my reason for writing to you before I meant to, is this.

The Bishop of Winchester and the Archbishop of York are not of one mind with the Archbishop of Canterbury. It is the old quarrel about the office of legate. But who are they and who is he? Is not the Archbishop of York that very person whom, in your presence when you were still in a manner one of us, your brethren resisted to the face because he was to blame? But he put his trust in the abundance of riches and, in the vanity of his heart, he has prevailed. . . . When you have time, deal with them according to their works, so that they may know a prophet has arisen in Israel.

To Pope Eugene III, Letter 238

With greater joy did Bernard write when brethren arrived bearing personal greetings from the new Pope.

"As cold water to a thirsty soul, so is good tidings from a far country." I received with joy, as coming from your presence, our brothers Gg. and G. and I was much consoled by all they told me. I had heard from others a little time before of this great event which has happened, of what the Lord has done to his child. But they did not bring your blessing with them. So when your letter bearing upon it your own seal was unrolled, from the fullness thereof we all received good tidings, words of consolation, the greeting and apostolic benediction. When I heard this, my spirit came to life within me and I cast myself prostrate on the ground in thanks to God, and your brethren and I all prostrated ourselves in your honor.
To Pope Eugene III, Letter 508

Street fountain in Conques.

Bernard did not hesitate to write to his "son" now become his "father" with great frankness.

Let others fear your majesty, so that with trembling lips and fingers and by devious circumlocutions they can hardly come to the point of what they want to say. I have regard only for your honor and advantage and say what I have to say openly and at once. I am not afraid to say what is necessary without any delay or beating about the bush, just as if you were one of ourselves. Therefore I do not hesitate to tell you that you have been deceived and very gravely.... There is nothing else for you to do but to revoke your decision.... It only remains for me to satisfy my own conscience by quoting to you those words, "Be angry and sin not." You will sin if you are not angry with the man who gave you this deceitful advice and inveigled from you such an unworthy decision.
Letter 268

Bernard's relationship with Pope Eugene was quite unique. After many years in office, the Pope still related to Bernard as his teacher. Bernard responds warmly to the Pope's request for his spiritual support and formal instruction.

It has occurred to me to write something which might edify, delight or console you, Blessed Father Eugene. But I do not know the rules for writing a formal yet intimate treatise. Two opposites, your majesty and my love, vie to dictate my style. Love draws me on; majesty holds me back. But you graciously intervene and request rather than command this treatise although it would be more fitting for you to command it. Since Your Majesty so admirably condescends, why does my hesitancy persist? What if you have ascended the throne? Even if you were to walk on the wings of the wind, you would not escape my affection. Love knows no master. It recognizes a son even though he wear the tiara. It is the nature of a lover to be suitably humble, willingly submissive, freely compliant, respectful with duress. . . . It is true that I have been freed of my maternal obligation toward you but I am not stripped of affection for you. You were once in my womb; you will not be drawn from my heart so easily. Ascend to the heavens, descend to the depths, you will not escape me. I shall follow you wherever you

go. I loved you when you were poor in spirit; I shall love you still as father of the poor and the rich. If I know you, you did not cease being poor in spirit when you became the father of the poor. I am confident that this change has been thrust upon you and was not of your doing, that this promotion had not replaced your former state, but rather has enhanced it. Therefore, I will instruct you not as a teacher, but as a mother, indeed, as a lover. I may seem more the fool but only to one who does not love, to one who does not feel the force of love.
On Consideration, Preface

Bernard found himself advising mystics and saints. Perhaps one of the best known of his time was St. Hildegard, the Abbess of Mount St. Rupert. Bernard responds to her effusive letter to him with considerable reserve.

To his beloved daughter in Christ, Hildegard, whatever the prayers of a sinner can avail, from Brother Bernard, Abbot of Clairvaux.

That others should believe me a better person than I know myself to be is due more to human stupidity than any special merits on my part. I hasten to reply to your sweet and kindly letter, although the multitude of my affairs obliges me to do so more briefly than I could wish. I congratulate you on the grace of God that is in you and admonish you to regard it as a gift and respond to it with all humility and devotion in the sure knowledge that God flouts the scornful and gives the humble his grace. This is what I beg and implore you to do. How could I presume to teach or advise you who are favored with hidden knowledge and in whom the influence of Christ's anointing still lives so that you have no need of teaching, for you are said to be able to search the secrets of heaven and to discern by the light of the Holy Spirit things that are beyond the knowledge of us humans? It is rather for me to beg that you may not forget me before God,

The Mill of Mysticism (capital). Basilica of St. Mary Magdalene, Vézelay.

or those who are united to me in spiritual fellowship. I am sure that when your spirit is united to God you could help and benefit us much, for when a just person prays fervently there is great virtue in her prayer. We pray without ceasing for you that you may be strengthened in all good, instructed in interior things and guided to what endures so that those who put their trust in God may not fall by losing faith in you but may rather derive strength so as to make ever greater progress in good from the sight of your own progress in the graces which you are known to have received from God.

Letter 366

An indication of the harshness of the times is the number of letters that Bernard wrote in regard to the violence done to clerics. Here, with biblical imagery appropriate to the horror of the crime, Bernard writes to the Pope about the murder in 1133 of Thomas, the Prior of St. Victor at Paris.

To his most loving father and lord, Innocent, by the grace of God Supreme Pontiff, the entire devotion and service, for what it is worth, of Bernard, the unworthy Abbot of Clairvaux.

A wild beast has devoured Joseph and, unable to meet the attacks of our dogs, he has fled to you, they say, for protection. The wretch must be mad to think that he, a wanderer and fugitive on earth, can find a refuge where he should have most cause for fear. The scoundrel! Does he think that the seat of supreme justice is a den of thieves or a lair of lions? Does he seek refuge with the mother whose son he has butchered? Does he dare to appear before his father, still licking his chops, his jaws still red with the blood of his son? If he should ask to do penance, it should not be denied him. But if he should only ask for a hearing, let him receive the answer that Moses gave to the people when they were worshipping the molten image or that Phinees gave to the fornicating Israelite or that Mattathias gave to the

Punished sinners are pushed into the jaws of a monster. Façade of the Basilica of St. Foy in Conques.

man who sacrificed to devils or, to take examples from nearer your home, let him hear from you what Ananias heard from the blessed Peter or what the Savior said to the money changers in the temple. Do we not know that the sins of some men go before them to judgment? Does not the voice of your brother's blood cry out against him to heaven? I believe that the spirit of our martyr, whom he has brutally killed during the last few days with the souls of all the others who have been slain, is crying out with a strong voice from beneath the altar and demanding a vengeance, all the more urgently for his blood having been poured forth so recently. . . .

Judge this man, my Lord and Father, as it shall seem good to you but let your judgment be such as to benefit the Church and assure security not only for the present time but for future generations. Let coming generations know not only of the crime that was done in our times but also of the punishment that rapidly followed.

To Pope Innocent II, Letter 158

Rightly then could Bernard be very critical of the clergy and especially of the hierarchs of his time, as in this letter to Pope Innocent II.

The insolence of the clergy is being everywhere a nuisance and troubling the whole Church. The cause of it is the negligence of the bishops. The bishops throw what is holy to the dogs and cast pearls before swine who turn upon them and tread them down. But it is only right that they should have to suffer for those they foster. Because they do not correct those whom they endow with the riches of the Church, they have to put up with their misconduct. The clergy fatten on the sweat of others, they devour the fruits of the earth without charge and so malice distills from their pampered lives. The old saying of Scripture is true today, "The people sat down to eat and drink and rose up to take their pleasure." The mind accustomed to delicate meats and uncultivated by the rake of discipline contracts much filth. And if you attempt to clean it away, they will not permit you to so much as touch it with your finger tips but act like those of whom Scripture says, "A people well loved and pampered would throw off the yoke and revolt against their deliverer."
Letter 152

Even as he criticizes, intercedes, and counsels, Bernard has great respect for bishops and for their authority.

In view of my own insignificance and the limits of my office I am always most careful not to overreach myself. . . . It would be exceedingly rash of me to undertake the functions of bishops, being myself no more than a sinner like other men and quite unskilled in all matters. When any serious question arises which either I do not know how to settle or cannot settle or do not dare to settle, like everyone else I refer it, as is only fitting, to the decision of the bishop. I am not easy about it until I have been fortified by his judgment or advice.

To Bishop Ricuin of Toul, Letter 61

In an age when bishops were usually elected by the clergy of the diocese it is not surprising that the choice fell on Bernard on more than one occasion: in his own diocese of Langres, at Milan to whom he had brought peace, and at Reims, to mention only three. In connection with the last-named election Bernard outlines in a letter to King Louis the Young the reasons he consistently refused the miter.

I am very glad you are so sincere in all that appertains to the glory of God. For, not to mention other things, you would surely not be so very anxious to promote such a wretched person as myself except for the glory of God. What other reason could you have since I am poor and destitute? You were not satisfied with simply consenting to my election [at Reims], you also added your request that I should accept it. You show me favor, you open wide to me your kind heart and, so that I should not be scared of the burden, you promise to help me with your royal protection. Whence such condescension in a king, such maturity in one so young? But, O King, I am a timorous character, broken in body and there only remains for me the grave. I cannot on any account stretch forth my hands to great works. Unfitted and unequal to such a holy office I cannot possibly venture to accept it. Those responsible for my election should have considered this.

If they are able to overlook my insufficiency, I cannot because I have read, "Your own self befriend, doing God's will." If they consider me suitable because of the religious habit I wear, they must understand that in the habit there is the appearance of holiness but not the virtue. No one is better known to me than myself, no one knows me so well as I know myself. I cannot believe against my conscience those who only see me from without and judge me only by appearances. I and the sons God has given me are here and, although sinners, we pray for your kingdom and your person. To part us would be difficult and cruel and would induce sorrow rather than prayers. So much for myself.

Now I beg you to deign to listen to what is in my mind about the church. [Bernard goes on to plead for the church he is refusing to rule.]

Letter 449

Bernard's warnings were many and varied. To a bishop called Alexander the Magnificent he wrote:

I feel impelled and even inspired by the Charity of God to exhort you not to regard the passing glory of the world as if it would never pass away and so lose the glory that endures forever. Do not love your possessions more than yourself or only for your own sake. Do not allow the flattery of present prosperity to hide from you the inevitable end so that when it comes it will bring endless adversity. Do not allow the pleasures of this world to beget for you and conceal from you the endless woe which they beget by concealing so that when you think death is far off, it may come upon you unawares. While you are counting on a long life, life itself may suddenly leave you, ill prepared according to what has been written: "It is just when men are saying: all is quiet, all is safe, that doom will fall upon them suddenly like the pangs of a woman in travail and there will be no escape from it."

To Bishop Alexander of Lincoln, Letter 64.3

Bernard stoutly upheld the principles of the Gregorian reform in regard to the plenitude of the papal authority within the Church. In a letter to the people of Milan, he sets it forth quite succinctly.

But someone may say: I will show the Roman Church due reverence but nothing more. So be it, do as you say. If you show the reverence that is due to it, it will be a reverence without reserve, for the Apostolic See, by a unique privilege, is endowed with a full authority over all the churches of the world. Anyone who withstands this authority sets his face against the decrees of God. The Apostolic See can, if it judges it expedient, set up new bishops where hitherto there have been none. Of those that already exist it can put down some and raise up others just as it judges best, so that if it deems it necessary it can raise bishops to be archbishops and the reverse. It can summon churchpersons, no matter how high and mighty they be, from the ends of the earth and bring them to its presence not just once or twice but as often as it sees fit.

Letter 131.2

Nonetheless, Bernard was aware of the limitations of the Pope and his fallibility. In a letter denouncing "a rebellious, proud and ambitious monk" who was seeking papal patronage, Bernard wrote:

This last Judas seems to have surpassed the first in cunning and deceit, as the first horrified all his co-apostles by his crime, whereas this one has been crafty enough to persuade not just anyone but the very chiefs of the apostles to wink at or rather to favor his wickedness. I do not blame my lord, the Pope. Like any other man he can be deceived. And I pray that God may not blame him. But may it be far from him to permit the execrable and sacrilegious endeavors of this evil person to prevail after he has learned the truth.

To the Bishops of Ostia, Tusculum, and Palestrina, Letter 231

During many of these years the Church was torn apart because of the election of a rival pope, Peter Leonis, who took the name Anacletus II. Bernard used his powerful pen as well as his persuasive presence to obtain the recognition of the true Pope, Innocent II. He mustered the arguments in favor of Innocent.

"A triple cord shall not be lightly broken." The choice of the most worthy of the Sacred College, the approbation of the majority of the people and (what is more than all this) the witness of a pure life, all combine to commend Innocent to everyone and establish him beyond doubt as the Supreme Pontiff.
To Hildebert of Tours, Letter 124.2

We have escaped the roaring of Peter the Lion [the antipope], only to encounter the hissing of Peter the Dragon. But you, Lord Jesus, will humble the proud with their haughty looks and tread under foot the Lion and the Dragon.
To Cardinal Guy, Letter 332

In a tireless campaign, he wrote letter after letter like this one to the bishops of Aquitaine, where he argues from the long list of those whom he has already won over.

God's word runs swiftly bringing people and kings together in one that they might serve and obey Pope Innocent. Who can appeal against this? It is recognized as the judgment of God by Walter of Ravenna, Hildegard of Tarragona, Norbert of Magdeburg, Conrad of Salzburg, all archbishops. It is known and accepted as the judgment of God by the bishops, Equipert of Münster, Hildebrand of Pistoia, Bernard of Pavia, Landulf of Asti, Hugh of Grenoble and Bernard of Parma. The singular prestige, the outstanding sanctity and authority of these prelates, respected even by their enemies, have easily persuaded me who occupy a lower position both in office and virtue to follow them whether right or wrong. I do not mention the great multitude of others, the archbishops and bishops of Tuscany, Campania, Lombardy, Germany, Aquitaine, of France, too, and all Spain, as well as the whole Eastern Church whose names are in the book of life but cannot find a place in a short letter.

All these men, with one accord, with no inducement of money, undeceived by any fallacy, not led by consideration of human relationship, nor under duress from civil power but with eyes fully open to God's will which they perceive most clearly, reject Peter Leonis and without any hesitation acclaim Gregory as Pope Innocent. Of our own prelates I do not mention one in this letter, because there is no space to mention all and to mention some would be invidious and expose me to suspicions of flattery. But I ought not to pass over those holy men who, being dead to this world, lead a better life to God alone, those whose life is hid with Christ in glory where they zealously seek and doubtless find what is the pleasure of God and whose only care is to please him. Of these the Camaldolese, Vallambrosians, Carthusians, Cluniacs, the brethren of Marmoutiers, my own Cistercians, the brethren of Caen, Tiron and Savigny, in a word all the brethren, both secular and regular, with unanimous accord adhere to Innocent, sincerely approve him, humbly obey him and loyally recognize him as the true successor of the Apostle.

What about the kings and princes of the world, are they not united in the same spirit together with their subjects, acclaiming Innocent and confessing him the Pope and bishop of their souls? What man is there of good repute and illustrious in any rank of life who does not believe the same?

To the Bishops of Aquitaine, Letter 126.9-10

He did not labor in vain. At this crossroads it is not an exaggeration to say that Bernard's role was decisive.

I, for my part, together with other servants of God aflame with the divine fire, am laboring with the help of God "to assemble the kings and people together" to break this conspiracy of evil men and destroy "every height that exalts itself against the knowledge of God." Nor have we labored in vain. The kings of Germany, France, England, Scotland, Spain and Jerusalem with all their clergy and people support and follow the Lord Innocent, as sons their father, as members their head. They zealously preserve unity in the bond of peace. The Church supports him with good reason, for it has learned that his reputation is more fair and his election more sound in that his supporters prevailed both in numbers and excellence.

To Geoffrey of Loreto, Letter 125.2

In the end he was completely victorious as he reports to his prior at Clairvaux.

To Brother Godfrey the greetings of Brother Bernard.

On the very day of Pentecost [May 29, 1138] God fulfilled our desires by giving unity to the Church and peace to the city of Rome. On that day all the supporters of Peter Leonis prostrated themselves at the feet of the Lord Pope to take the oath of fealty and become his liege men. And the clergy who had been in schism, together with the idol they had set up [Victor, the antipope who succeeded Anacletus], also prostrated themselves at the feet of our Lord the Pope and according to the custom promised him obedience. There was great joy among the people. At last the peace has come which I felt so sure would come though I could not tell when it would come. Now nothing remains to keep me here any longer and I can change "I will come" for "I am coming," as you have been imploring me to do.

Letter 317

The papal schism was not long settled when Bernard, advised and urged by his theologian friend, William of St. Thierry, began to employ the full power of his rhetoric to bring to an end what he considered the pernicious influence of Peter Abelard. In this he demonstrated his devotion to the theological heritage of the Church as well as his considerable power within the Church, but also perhaps a lack of openness to possible new ways of theological development. In the heat of argument he also does violence to the person of Abelard. Bernard's initial reply indicates his diffidence to enter into the fray.

To his dear friend William from Brother Bernard.

In my opinion your misgivings are well called-for and reasonable. This is evident from your booklet [William's own "Response to the Errors of Abelard"] in which you bruise and close the lips that utter wickedness. Not that I have yet had the opportunity to read it with the attention you require. But from what I have been able to see by glancing through it I like it very much and consider it well able to overthrow the iniquitous teaching. As you well know, I am not in the habit of trusting much my own judgment especially in such grave matters as these, so I suggest that it would be worth our while to meet somewhere as soon as you have the opportunity and discuss the whole thing. But I do not think this can be arranged before Easter lest we are distracted from the prayer that is proper to this season of Lent. I beg you, in the meantime, to suffer patiently my own patience and silence, for at present I know little or nothing at all of these matters. Yet in answer to your prayers God can give me the power for what you are urging me to do. Farewell.

To William, Abbot of St. Thierry, Letter 327

After studying the matter, Bernard wrote with his usual verve to the Curia at Rome.

The faith of the simple is being held up to scorn, the secrets of God are being ripped open, the most sacred matters are being recklessly discussed and the Fathers are being derided because they held that such matters are better allowed to remain intact than that efforts be made to tear them open. Hence it has come about that, contrary to the law of God, the Paschal Lamb is either boiled or eaten raw, with bestial mouth and manners. And what is left over is not burned with fire but trodden under foot. Mere human ingenuity is taking on itself to solve everything and leave nothing to faith. It is striving for things above itself, prying into things too potent for it, rushing into divine things and profaning rather than revealing what is holy. Things closed and sealed it is not opening but tearing asunder and what it is not able to force open that it considers to be of no account and not worthy of belief.

Read if you please that book of Peter Abelard which he calls a book of theology. You have it to hand since, as he boasts, it is read eagerly by many in the Curia. See what sort of things he says there about the Holy Trinity, about the generation of the Son, about the procession of the Holy Spirit and much else that is very strange indeed to Catholic ears and minds. Read that other book which they call the *Book of Sentences* and also the one entitled *Know Yourself* and see how they, too, run riot with a whole crop of sacrileges and errors. See what he thinks about the soul of Christ, about the person of Christ, about his descent into hell, about the Sacrament of the Altar, about the power of binding and loosing, about original sin, about the sins of human weakness, about sins of ignorance, about sinful action and about sinful intention. And if you then consider that I am rightly disturbed, do you also bestir yourselves and so as not to bestir yourselves in vain, act according to the position you hold, according to the dignity in which you are supreme, according to the power you have received. Let him who has scanned the heavens go down even into hell and let the works of darkness that have braved the light be shown up by the light, so that while he who sins in public is publicly rebuked, others who speak evil in their hearts and write it in their books may restrain themselves from putting darkness for light and disputing on divine matters at the crossroads. . . .

Letter 188

Chapter House of Sens Cathedral in Sens, France.

After the meeting of the Church at Sens, Bernard wrote his account of it to Pope Innocent II.

At Abelard's request the Archbishop of Sens wrote to me fixing the day of the meeting in which Abelard, in the Archbishop's presence and in the presence of his brother bishops, should establish, if he could, his perverse doctrines against which I have dared to croak. I refused because I am but a child in this sort of warfare and he is a man habituated to it from his youth and because I deemed it an unworthy action to bring the faith into the arena of controversy, resting as it does on sure and immutable truth. I said that his writings were evidence enough against him and that it was the business of the bishops to adjudicate on doctrines of which they were the ministers, not mine. But he lifted up his voice all the more for this meeting, called upon many, and assembled all his accomplices. I would rather not say what he wrote about me to his disciples. He spread it about on all sides that he was going to answer me at Sens on the day appointed. The word of it went forth to everyone and I was not able to hide myself. At first I did nothing, not greatly caring for what people were saying. Yet, unwillingly and sorrowfully, I bowed to the advice of my friends who saw how everyone was preparing as if for a show and feared that my absence would serve only to increase the influence of the man and the scandal of the people. Also it seemed that his errors might appear to be confirmed if there were no one to answer and refute them. And so I went to Sens at the time appointed, unprepared, unprotected except by those words which I had in my mind at the time, "Take no thought how or what to speak, for it will be given you in that hour what to speak" and "With the Lord to aid me, I have no fear of the worst man can do." Besides the bishops and abbots, there were many religious present and also the masters of the schools from the cities and many educated clerics. The king, too, was there. And so, in the presence of all, face to face with my adversary, I took certain headings from his books. And when I began to read these, he refused to listen and walked out and appealed from the judges he had chosen, which I do not think was permissible. When the headings from his books had been examined, they were found by the judgment of all to be contrary to the faith, to the truth. I have written all this on my own behalf in case I should be thought to have shown levity or at least rashness in so grave a matter.

Letter 189

After writing to the Pope, Bernard sent out a whole spate of letters to those around the Pope to assure the condemnation of the theologian. His letter to Guy (Guido in Italian), the cardinal priest who would become Pope Celestine II in 1143, is typical.

To his venerable Lord and most dear father, Master Guy, by the grace of God Cardinal Priest of the Holy Roman Church that he may not swerve either to the right or to the left, from Bernard, Abbot of Clairvaux.

I do not accuse Abelard before the Father, there is that book of his in which he takes such mistaken pleasure to accuse him. When he speaks of the Trinity, he savors of Arius; when of grace, he savors of Pelagius; when of the person of Christ, he savors of Nestorius. I do not question at all your judgment in the cause of Christ, having for so long begged you not to prefer anyone to Christ. But know this, that it is expedient for you to whom power has been given by the Lord, expedient for the Church of Christ and expedient for the man himself that silence should be imposed upon him because "his mouth overflows with curses and calumny and deceit, his tongue is a storehouse of misery and shame."

Letter 192

Peter Abelard proves by his life, by his behavior, by his books, which are now issuing from darkness into the light of day, that he is a persecutor of the Catholic Church and an enemy of the cross of Christ. Outwardly he appears as a monk, but within he is a heretic having nothing of the monk about him save the habit and name. He opens up the old wells and the trodden-in pools of heretics so that the ox and ass may fall in. He had long been silent but while he kept silence in Brittany he conceived sorrow and now in France he has brought forth iniquity. He has come out of his hole like a twisting snake and, like the hydra, when one head is cut off he grows seven more in its place. A single head was cut off, a single heresy of that man, at Soissons; but already seven greater ones have grown up in its place, an example of which I have sent to you. Raw and inexperienced listeners hardly finished with their dialectics and those who can hardly, so to speak, understand the first elements of the faith are introduced by him to the mystery of the Holy Trinity, to the Holy of Holies, to the chamber of the King and to him who is "shrouded with darkness." In fine, our theologian has laid down degrees and grades in the Trinity like Arius, with Pelagius he puts free will before grace and with Nestorius he divides Christ by excluding from association with the Trinity the human nature he assumed. He runs through almost all the sacraments and "boldly sweeps from the world's end to the world's end," ordering all things mischievously.

To Stephen, Cistercian Cardinal Bishop of Palestrina, Letter 331

We have in France one Peter Abelard, a monk without a rule, a prelate without responsibility, an abbot without discipline, who argues with boys and consorts with women. He puts "stolen waters and hidden bread" before his household in his books and in his discourses he introduces profane novelties of phrase and meaning. He approaches the dark cloud which surrounds God not alone as Moses did but with a whole crowd of his disciples. Catholic faith, the childbearing of the Virgin, the Sacrament of the Altar, the incomprehensible mystery of the Holy Trinity are being discussed in the streets and market places.

To Cardinal Guy, Letter 332

Even though Bernard vehemently attacked the "new theology" and for the moment decided the conservative direction the Church would take theologically, it would be wrong to see him as opposed to learning and serious study. He had salutary advice to give to scholars.

Perhaps you think that I have sullied too much the good name of knowledge, that I have cast aspersions on the learned and proscribed the study of letters. God forbid! I am not unmindful of the benefits its scholars conferred and still confer on the Church both by refuting her opponents and instructing the simple. And I have read the text: "As you have rejected knowledge so do I reject you from my priesthood" and that "the learned will shine as brightly as the vault of heaven and those who have instructed many in virtue as bright as stars for all eternity." But I recall reading, too, that knowledge puffs up. . . .

All knowledge is good in itself provided it be founded on truth, but since because of the brevity of time you are in a hurry to work out your salvation in fear and trembling, take care to learn principally and primarily the doctrines on which your salvation is more intimately dependent. Do not doctors of medicine hold that the work of healing depends on a right choice in the taking of food, what to take first, what next, and the amount

of each to be eaten? Although it is clear that all the foods that God has made are good, if you fail to take the right amount in due order, you obviously take them to the detriment of your health. What I say about foods I want you to apply to the various kinds of knowledge.
On the Song of Songs, 36.2

While Bernard appreciated learning rightly pursued and rightly used, he appreciated even more that knowledge and wisdom that comes from the Holy Spirit. When Aelred, the Abbot of Rievaulx, a monastery started by Bernard in what was then Scotland, expressed his reluctance to write a treatise on love, Bernard wrote to him.

You have said that you are ignorant of grammar, that you are almost illiterate, that you have come from the desert, not from the schools but from the kitchen; that you have since lived a rustic and rough life amid rocks and mountains, earning in the sweat of your brow your daily bread with axe and maul and that flights of oratory ill become your poor fishermen's clothes. I most gratefully accept your excuses. They serve rather to inflame than to extinguish the spark of my desire, because knowledge that comes from the school of the Holy Spirit rather than the schools of rhetoric will savor all the sweeter to me and because you have this treasure in an earthen vessel so that the splendor of it may be of God.

What a joyous thing it is, what a promise for the future, that you should have come to the desert from the kitchen, so that as one who has been entrusted for a time with providing food for the body in a royal kitchen, you may

Tintern Abbey, a twelfth-century Cistercian monastery in Wales, Great Britain.

now provide spiritual food for spiritual men and feed the hungry with the food of God's word in the house of the King of Kings.

What you say about your mountains and rugged rocks does not disconcert me at all, nor am I put off at the thought of your great valleys, for now "the mountain drops down sweetness, the hills flow with milk and honey and the valleys are filled with corn," now "honey is sucked out of rocks and oil out of the hardest stone" and rocks and mountains are the pasture of the Lord's sheep. So I think that with that maul of yours you will be able to bring something out of those rocks that you would not have gotten by your own wits from the bookshelves of the schoolmen. You will have experienced at times under the shade of a tree during the heat of midday what you would never have learned in the schools.

Bernard's Prefatory Letter to Aelred's Mirror of Charity, Letter 523

Even while he actively championed the cause of unity and orthodoxy in the universal Church Bernard was an active leader in his own expanding Order. Besides the annual general chapter, which in principle brought all the Cistercian abbots together at Cîteaux, the Cistercian reform introduced an ongoing relationship between the abbey (called the motherhouse) that sent forth a group of monks to establish a new monastery and that new monastery (called the daughterhouse). The abbot of the motherhouse, besides the duty of making an annual visitation to the daughterhouse, had a certain undefined authority within the houses it had founded or which had been united to it as daughterhouses. This authority depended in good part on the charism of the abbot of the motherhouse. In the case of St. Bernard it was considerable and while it made great demands on him it gave him the opportunity to exercise a powerful presence in all parts of Christendom as Clairvaux's daughterhouses grew in number to sixty-eight.

The details were many and sometimes quite complicated in launching a new community of monks. Arrangements had to be made with the benefactors and with the local rulers; men had to be chosen and a superior prepared for them. This letter to the abbot of one daughterhouse, soliciting assistance in arranging for another, gives some hint of the possible complications.

I beg you to send for us to Montpellier either your father or some other intelligent messenger, so that he should arrive there on the octave of the Assumption of the Blessed Mary. For on that day, and in that place, there ought to be messengers from the King of Sicily, who "go down to the sea in ships" in order to bring the daughter of Count Theobald to the son of their lord. But if perchance they should have brought ships for our brothers and ask for the community we were to send them, then your messenger will excuse us in these words: "The brothers were ready and the community prepared, but the Lord Alfan, the messenger of the King of Sicily, said that the king only required two brothers, who were to go ahead of the others and see the place. But when it should please the king, he will make known to us his will concerning the sending of the whole community, since it is dangerous for the Order and for religion that brothers should live in a strange land without discipline and without the protection of either their abbot or their brethren.
To Amadeus, Abbot of Hautecombe, Letter 279

Facing page: An example of a place in the Rhône Valley in France, suitable for the establishment of a new Cistercian monastery "far removed from the turmoil of the world."

Bernard writes to his good friend Archbishop Malachy about the first foundation in Ireland.

To the venerable Lord and most blessed Father, Malachy, by the grace of God Archbishop of Ireland and Apostolic Legate, that he may find favor before God, from Bernard, Abbot of Clairvaux.

With regard to your wish that I should send you two of the brothers to prepare a place, I have discussed it with the brethren and we are agreed that it would not be well for them to be separated from us until Christ is more fully formed in them, until they are better equipped to fight for the Lord. When they have been instructed in the school of the Holy Spirit, when they are clothed with strength from on high, then they will return to their father to sing the songs of the Lord no longer in a strange land but in their own.

Do you in the meantime with the wisdom given you by the Lord look for and prepare a site similar to what you have seen here, far removed from the turmoil of the world.

Letter 341

But even with two saints engaged in bringing the foundation into being there were difficulties.

Concerning the brethren who have returned, I would have been well contented for them to have remained with you. But perhaps those natives of your country who are little disciplined and who found it hard to obey observances that were strange to them, may have been in some measure the occasion of their return.

I have sent back to you my very dear Christian, having instructed him as well as I could in the observances of our Order and I think that in the future he will be more careful about them. Do not be surprised that I have not been able to send many with him, for I could not find suitable men who were willing to go and I was loath to oblige them to do so against their will. My dear brother Robert acceded to my request this time like an obedient son. It will be your business to help him with the buildings and other things necessary for the well-being of the house. I would also suggest that you persuade those religious who you are hoping will be useful to the new monastery that they should unite with our Order, for this would be very advantageous to the house and you would be better obeyed. Farewell and always remember me in Christ.

To Archbishop Malachy, Letter 357

Bernard found it hard to send his spiritual sons forth and be separated from them. So he writes to the King of Sicily as he sends a group to start a house in his kingdom.

If you are seeking me, here I am with the children God has given me. It is said that my humble person has found such favor with your Royal Majesty that you desire to see me. And who am I to disregard the good pleasure of a king? I hasten to you and here am I whom you seek, not in weak bodily presence, the presence in which Herod mocked the Lord, but in my children, for who can separate me from them? Wherever they go, I will follow them. If they should come to rest at the furthest ends of the sea, there shall I be with them. You have, O King, the light of my eyes. You have my heart and my soul. What does it matter if the least part of me is absent? I mean my poor bit of a body, that wretched slave which my soul would gladly relinquish, did not necessity retain it. It cannot follow the willing soul because it is weak and the tomb is almost all there is left for it. But why care? "My soul shall dwell in joy while my seed shall inherit the land." My seed is good seed. It will bear fruit if it falls on good land. My soul shall be filled with joy because I trust it will receive the fruit of its labor. This is the hope laid up in my heart so that I can patiently bear to be parted even from these my sons. Do not wonder, O King. I would sooner have been parted from my body than separated from these, if God alone had not been the reason. Receive them as strangers and pilgrims, yet nevertheless as fellow citizens of the saints and of God's household. Rather I should say not merely citizens but kings, for by right and title of poverty theirs is the kingdom of heaven.

To Roger, King of Sicily, Letter 208

Bernard continued to follow the vicissitudes of his daughterhouses with great interest and care. In providing a good abbot for Fountains he had to deprive himself of the company of a close friend and find an abbot for another house.

To his very dear brother, Abbot Henry, greetings and prayer, from Bernard, Abbot of Clairvaux.

I charge you, Brother Henry, that you submit out of charity to the choice of our brothers of Fountains if, with the advice of the venerable Abbot of Rievaulx [St. Aelred], they elect you as their abbot. I do this very unwillingly, knowing that by your absence a great comfort will be lost to me. But I am afraid of resisting the choice of our brethren at Fountains, since I believe that when so many religious agree together their decision is the will of God, according to the words I read in the Gospel, "Where two or three are gathered together in my name, there am I in the midst of them." So stir yourself, dearest brother, and receive their professions of obedience and care for them as the shepherd of their souls. Have no fear for the house which you have been ruling [Vauclair]. It is quite near to me so, God willing, I shall be able to see that it has a capable administrator. And do not hesitate for the sake of the bishop, you can leave that to me.

To Henry Murdac, Letter 321

Bernard's labors for the Church universal as well as his poor health put limits on what he could do for his many daughterhouses. Oftentimes he was not even able to fulfill the primary duty of the Father Immediate (as the abbot of the motherhouse was called), that is, making the annual visitation, and had to delegate this to another.

To his very dear brothers in Christ and fellow abbots, William of Rievaulx and Richard of Fountains, and all the others united with them in the same necessity, that they may preserve unity of spirit in the bonds of peace, from Bernard, Abbot of Clairvaux.

"Who will give me the wings of a dove that I may go up to the people of ours who are girded for battle," that I may behold the joy of your fraternal love, that I may take my share in the troubles that abound in your place of pilgrimage, that I may save those who "perish from fears and the storms around them"? I am obliged to go out of my house on visitations by the rule of our Order, by the duty of our fraternity. . . . In this my heart would be filled as with some rich feast and in such things is the life of my spirit. For this I wait and wait, hoping to be given strength to follow my ready will but up to now I have been prevented. The way is hard and difficult and my body is weak. On top of all this, apart from my own weakness, the journeying I have to make on the business of my brethren and in the cause of the Church tower high above my head and land on me like a heavy burden. Because of this, Beloved, I am sending for your visitation my brother and dear friend, Henry, Abbot of Vauclair. Hear him, I beg you, as if he were myself. He is an upright and reasonable man who has taken on his shoulders some of my own cares and burdens and shares my powers for the correction of faults and the maintenance of the Order.

For the rest, as we all offend in many things and being often among men pick up much dust from the world, I commend myself, dearest brethren, to your prayers and those of your friends. You must throw me a rope of prayer, for I am laboring far out to sea while you are safe in port. I believe that at the word of the Lord the winds and the seas will be still. But he sleeps and you must waken him with your prayers.

Letter 535

While Bernard was compelled or impelled in his more mature years to respond to the needs of the Church he always returned gratefully to what he considered his primary vocation, that of abbot of his monks. At the end of the papal schism he wrote:

On this third return from Rome, my brothers, a more merciful eye has looked down from heaven. The Lion's [that is, the antipope's] rage has cooled, wickedness has ceased, the Church has found peace. The reprobate, the man who for almost eight years has bitterly embroiled it in schism, has been brought to nothing in its sight. But have I returned from so great dangers to be useless to you? I have been granted to your desires; I am ready to serve your advancement. Through your merits I am still alive, so I wish to live for your welfare, for your salvation.

On the Song of Songs, 24.1

Bernard bemoaned the fact that he had so often to be away from his cloister.

Ah! Happy are those who during evil times are hidden in the house of the Lord, who under the shadow of his wings are able to await in hope their passing. As for me, unhappy man, naked and poor, it is my lot to labor. An unfledged nestling, I am obliged to spend most of my time out of my nest exposed to the tempests and troubles of the world. I am shaken and upset like a drunken man and cares devour my conscience. So once more I say have pity on me who certainly need it even if I do not deserve it.

To Guy, Prior of the Carthusians, Letter 12

The Garden at the restored twelfth-century Cistercian Monastery of Notre Dame in Aigues Belle, Provence.

He repeatedly tried to put off the demands that were made upon him. He wanted to stay home in his cloister.

It is not laziness but a very much better reason that prevented me from coming when you sent for me. The truth is, saving your reverence and the reverence due to all good men, I have determined never to leave my monastery except for certain reasons none of which could be invoked on this occasion, as a pretext for satisfying your wishes and, indeed, my own. It would give me great pleasure if, mere rustic though I be, I could satisfy your wishes, for I am much in love with all I hear of you and I have a great respect for your care and zeal in the things of God.

To Cardinal Peter, Letter 17

FIVE
Walking Through His Own Times

Long after the inauguration of the Gregorian reform, Church and civil society continued to struggle to work out a meaningful coexistence. Bernard, *vir ecclesiasticus par excellence*, was often the mediator among princes as well as for princes even while he sought to harness the allegiance of princes to the cause of the Church. He wholeheartedly accepted the theory of the two swords: the sword of the spirit wielded by the Church and the sword of temporal power wielded by the state but subject to the call of the Church. Bernard successfully called forth this latter sword to finally settle Innocent II peacefully on his papal throne after a long struggle with an antipope and his allies.

Again Bernard called it forth in the tragic drama of the Second Crusade. If there is any aspect of the career of this blessed man of peace that is hard for the modern to understand, it is Bernard's role as the animator of the Second Crusade. Maybe the crusade's failures are a sign that his peaceful heart was not fully in it. His symbolic theology nonetheless wholly supported it. The "infidels" were seen too clearly as the forces of evil. The crusaders were, in an age highly enamored with the ideal of the pilgrimage, ultimately only pilgrims who were armed to defend their fellow pilgrims from the forces of evil. The hands of the clock of history again reached the hour that marked a clash of East and West; Bernard helped to powerfully cloth this clash in religious garb. The garb did not hold when the Christian East failed to align with the Christian West and even the

Christian West fell apart. The great borders did not shift much in the course of the succeeding centuries. Bernard's faith-full rationalizations to explain the failure of his crusade covered all the succeeding failures as well.

Although Bernard suffered disappointment and defeat he never ceased to be a concerned pilgrim, always filled with concern for those who walked with him on the journey of life. He did not allow the overriding concern of the Second Crusade to prevent him from responding to a cry for help from the Jews of the Rhineland. When he heard an erratic monk was seeking to lead a misguided "crusade" against the children of Abraham, Bernard went quickly to their aid. Even from his deathbed he rose in the cause of peace to bring reconciliation to the warring factions in Lorraine. This last mission was a complete success and Bernard's journey home — to die — was a march of triumph, or rather a stately procession surrounded by venerating crowds as he passed along the Moselle through Gondreville and Toul to Clairvaux.

A contemplative at the heart of the world, Bernard's love and care reached out to all the world with its many concerns. He respected all vocations.

The Church's robe is many-colored because of the many different religious orders that are distinguished in it. It is seamless because of the undivided unity of love that cannot be torn apart. As it is written: "Who will separate us from the love of Christ?" First, hear how the robe is many-colored: "There are varieties of graces but the same Spirit; there are different works but the same Lord." Then, after listing the various charisms which correspond to the different hues of the many-colored robe, the Apostle adds the following to show that it is also seamless, woven from top to bottom: "All these are the work of the one and the same Spirit, proportionate to each as he pleases. For love has been poured forth in our hearts by the Holy Spirit who has been given to us."

Therefore, let there be no division within the Church. Let it remain whole and entire according to its inherited right. Concerning the Church it has been written: "At your right hand the queen in a golden robe, interlaced with variety." This is why different people receive different gifts. One is allotted one kind, one another, irrespective of whether he be a Cistercian or Cluniac, a regular or one of

the laity. This applies to every order and to all languages, to both sexes, to every age and condition of life.
Apologia 6

Yet Bernard saw the vocation to serve God in the clerical order as distinct from the call to serve in the civil sphere.

Who would not be indignant, who would not deplore, even if only in secret, that a man should against the Gospel both serve God as a deacon and Mammon as a minister of state, that he should be so loaded with ecclesiastical honors as to seem hardly inferior to the bishops while being at the same time so involved in military affairs as to take precedence over the commanders of the army? I ask you what sort of monster is this that being a cleric wishes to be thought a soldier as well? And succeeds in being neither. It is an abuse of both conditions that a deacon should serve the table of a king and that a servant of the king should minister at the holy mysteries of the altar. Who would not be astonished or rather disgusted that one and the same person would, arrayed in armor, lead soldiers in battle and, clothed in alb and stole, pronounce the Gospel in the church; should at one time give signal for battle on the bugle and at another inform the people of the commands of the bishop?
To Abbot Suger of St. Denis, Letter 78.11

Bernard was one of the strong proponents of the theory of the "two swords." As he wrote to Pope Eugene III:

The person who denies that the sword is yours seems to me not to listen to the Lord when he says, "Sheathe your sword." Therefore, this sword is yours and is to be drawn from its sheath at your command, although not by your hand. Otherwise, if that sword in no way belongs to you, the Lord would not have answered, "That is enough," but "That is too much," when the Apostles said, "Behold, here are two swords." Both swords, that is, the spiritual and the material, belong to the Church. The spiritual sword should be drawn by the hand of the priest; the material sword by the hand of the knight, but clearly at the bidding of the priest and at the command of the emperor.
On Consideration, 4.7

Nonetheless, Bernard saw Church and State intimately united in Christ. The people are the one People of God.

The Crown and the Church could not be more sweetly, more cordially or more closely united and grafted together than in the person of the Lord since he came to us according to the flesh from the royal and priestly tribes as both our king and our high priest. And not only this but he has also so mingled and combined both these characters in his body, which is the Christian people, with himself their head that the Apostle [St. Paul] calls this race of persons "a chosen generation, a kingly priesthood." And in another part of the Scriptures are not all those predestined to life called kings and priests? Therefore what God has joined together let no one put asunder. Let us rather try to concur with the divine plan by uniting ourselves in spirit with those to whom we are united by constitution. Let us cherish each other, defend each other and carry each other's burdens, for Solomon says, "When brother helps brother, theirs is the strength of a fortress." But if they both snarl and snap at each other, they will both be destroyed. May I have no part in the counsels of those who say either that the peace and liberty of the Church will suffer from the empire or that the prosperity and glory of the empire will suffer from the Church. For God who founded both did not unite them for their mutual destruction but for their mutual support.

To Conrad, King of the Romans, Letter 244

Bernard sometimes used his influence as friend and counselor to call forth the secular sword in service of the Church.

To Lothair, by the grace of God Emperor of Rome and Augustus, the prayers of a sinner for what they are worth, from Bernard, Abbot of Clairvaux.

Blessed be God who has raised you up to be a scepter of salvation among us for the honor and glory of his name, to restore the imperial dignity, to support the Church in an evil hour and finally to work salvation even now upon the earth. It is his doing that the power of your crown spreads and rises more each day, ever increasing and growing in dignity and splendor before God and men. It was certainly by his strength and power that you were able to make such successful progress in the difficult and dangerous journey you undertook for the peace of your kingdom and the liberation of the Church. You have magnificently achieved the full summit of imperial dignity and what is more the greatness of your soul. Faith shone out all the more clearly from your having achieved this with no great show of power. If the earth trembled and was silent before so tiny an army, how much more will terror seize upon the heart of the enemy when the king begins to show that full strength of his arm! The goodness of his cause will inspire him and a double necessity will urge him. It is not any of my business to incite to a battle but I do say, without hesitation, that it is the concern of a friend of the Church to save it from the mad fury of the schismatics. . . . I am but an insignificant person, but I am your friend, so that, if I should seem importunate it is perhaps because of that. I send my devoted greetings in Christ to her Imperial Royal Highness the Empress.

To Emperor Lothair, Letter 139

Bernard often found himself in the presence of the high and powerful leaders of his time and frequently wrote to them to give them guidance and direction. He truly desired their well-being and that of their realms and people, yet he did not hesitate to be very frank.

To Louis, by the grace of God illustrious King of France and Duke of Aquitaine, that he may love righteousness and judge his land with wisdom, from Bernard, Abbot of Clairvaux.

Though all the world were to combine in making me attempt something against your Royal Majesty, yet I would fear God and not dare to oppose the king whom he had ordained. I know where it is written, "He that resists the power, resists the ordinance of God." But I shall speak the truth to you because I also know how wrong it is for any Christian to lie, especially for one of my profession. . . .

I would rather die than see a king of such a fair reputation and of even better hopes attempt to oppose the will of God and stir up against himself the wrath of the supreme Judge, bathe the feet of the Father of Orphans in the tears of the afflicted, cause the portals of heaven to resound with the cries of the poor, the prayers of the saints and the just complaints of the chaste Bride of Christ who is the Church of the Living God. May God forbid such a thing! We hope for better things, we expect more joyful things of you. God will not forget to be merciful nor will his wrath set bounds to his pity. He will not permit his Church to be saddened through the king and on account of the king by whom he has already given her such joy on so many occasions. And if you think otherwise, this also he will reveal to you, schooling your heart in wisdom. This is our wish and our prayer day and night. Believe this of me and believe it of my brethren. This truth will never be denied by us and the honor of our king and the welfare of his realm will never be diminished by us.

Letter 170

Bernard addressed the leaders of republican government. In 1133 Bernard brought about a treaty of peace between Pisa and Genoa who had been at war for more than fifty years. The next year he wrote to the people of Genoa:

To the Consuls, Councilors and all the people of Genoa, peace, health and eternal life, from Bernard, Abbot of Clairvaux.

I brought to you words of peace and, finding you the sons of peace, I left my peace with you. I went forth to sow seed, God's seed, not mine, and the good seed I sowed fell on good ground yielding a hundredfold with wonderful speed, because the necessity was great. I experienced no difficulty or delay but almost on one and the same day I both sowed and reaped, returning with joy as I carried with me the sheaves of peace. And this was the harvest I reaped: a joyous hope of release and home for men in captivity, chains and prison and fear for our enemies, disgrace for the schismatics, glory for the Church and great joy for everyone.

Preserve peace with your brothers and sisters of Pisa, faith with the Lord Pope, loyalty to the King and honor among yourselves. This is desirable, becoming and just.

Letter 129

Although he readily acknowledged his limitations, Bernard was happy to be called upon to serve in the cause of peace. After winning them over to the side of Pope Innocent in 1135, Bernard wrote to the people of Milan.

I learn from your letters that I enjoy some favor with you. But, as I can find no reason for this in myself, I must attribute it to a gift of God. I do not refuse the favor of such a great people, on the contrary I willingly accept it and devotedly embrace with open arms the devotion of so renowned a city, especially now that you have cast aside schism and, to the joy of everyone, have returned to the bosom of the Church. It is a matter of great satisfaction to myself that I should have been invited to negotiate the peace; that, although a poor person of no consequence, I should yet have been asked to assume the role of ambassador in such an excellent cause. And I consider it not a little to your honor that you should be ready to be turned to peace with your neighbors by such a person as myself when, as everyone knows, the hostile invasions of many cities have been powerless to force this on you. I am now hastening to the Council [the Council of Pisa, which was held from May 26 through June 5, 1135] but I propose to visit you on the way back so as to experience the good will of which you assure me. May God who has inspired you thus to use me grant that you may not do so in vain!

Letter 133

Bernard did not hesitate at times to approach kings and queens, nobles and knights on behalf of his own needs and those of his Order. He writes to the Queen of Jerusalem on behalf of a young relative.

They say that I have some influence with you and many who are to set out for Jerusalem beg me to commend them to Your Excellency. Among them is this

The Citadel of Jerusalem was built on the basis of the Crusader Citadel in Jerusalem, Israel.

young man, a kinsman of mine, a youth strong, they say, in arms and polished in manners. And I am delighted that for the time being he has chosen to fight for God rather than for the world. Act according to your custom and for my sake see that all is well with him as it has been for all my other kinsmen who were able to introduce themselves to you by means of myself. . . . And if it is true what my dear Uncle Andrew says of you — and he is a man in whom I have every confidence — you will reign by the mercy of God both here and in eternity. Take care of the pilgrims, the needy and especially the prisoners, for God is gained by such sacrifices. Write to me often because it will not hurt you and it will benefit me to know fully and for certain of your state and dispositions.
To Queen Melisande, Letter 206

The Citadel of Provins, the residence of the Count of Troyes. Clairvaux was on the lands of the Count of Troyes.

Bernard found time to concern himself about the temporal well-being of individuals. He could even concern himself about a flock of pigs.

The Abbot of Châtillon, a good man, when he set out for Rome left all his property under my protection. And now the servants of Simon, men of Belfort, have taken off with his pigs. I assure you I would rather have had my own pigs stolen. The King of Kings has set you up as a prince upon earth so that by his power and for his sake you may encourage the good, restrain the evil, defend the poor and give justice to those who suffer injuries. If you do this you will be fulfilling the functions of your state and can have every reason to hope that God will increase and strengthen your principality. But if you fail to do this it is much to be feared that the very honor and power which you seem to have may be taken away from you. May God forbid such a thing!

To Count Henry of Champagne, Letter 279

Bernard could also give advice on what seems to be matters far from his affairs as a monk. Here he counsels a mother on how to raise her son.

I am sorry your son has behaved badly toward you. I deplore as much the conduct of the son as the wrong done to his mother. Yet, after all, such conduct is excusable in a young son. Youth is ever prone to such faults and is itself an excuse for them. Do you not realize that all the thoughts and imaginations of a man's heart are bent toward evil from youth? You may be sure that the merits and alms of his father will bring about a change for the better in him. You must offer more and more vows and prayers to God for him because, even though at the moment his conduct toward you is not what it should be, yet nevertheless a mother ought not and cannot lose her maternal affection for her children. "Can a mother ever forget the son she bore in her womb?" asks the Prophet. And he adds, "Even if she were to forget, I will not be forgetful of you." The young man has so many excellent qualities that we must offer prayers and tears to the Lord that God may enable him (as I am sure he will) to emulate the goodness of his father. He must be treated with gentleness and kindly forbearance because by such treatment he will be more encouraged to do good than if he were exasperated by nagging and scolding. I am

sure that by these means we will soon be able to rejoice over a happy change in him. There is nothing I desire more than that he should change for the better. I wish I could find his conduct toward others as irreproachable as I have always found it toward myself, for I have never known him to be anything but most ready and willing to do all I wished. May God reward him for this! But as you asked me to do, I am always remonstrating with him about his conduct toward you and I shall continue to do so.
To the Countess of Blois, Letter 300

Beginning at Vézelay on March 31, 1146, Bernard received a good response to his preaching.

You have commanded and I have obeyed. The authority of your command has made my obedience fruitful. Since I have announced and have spoken, the soldiers of the Cross have been increased beyond number. Cities and castles are emptied and now seven women can hardly find one man to hold, so much so that everywhere there are widows whose husbands are still alive.

To Pope Eugene III, Letter 248

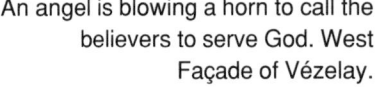

An angel is blowing a horn to call the believers to serve God. West Façade of Vézelay.

In obedience to the Pope in 1146 Bernard began to promote the Second Crusade. On Easter, Bernard preached for the first time to the wide public of French nobles including Louis VII, King of France, at Vézelay. In fact, there were so many people who attended Bernard's sermon that the large basilica was too small, and all gathered outside on the slope.

The Cordelier, the slope outside the Church of Vézelay, where Bernard preached the Second Crusade to the crowds that assembled on Easter, 1146.

The original sermon is lost. We do have letters, however, which he later wrote in the same spirit to the people of East Francia and Bavaria.

To the very lords and fathers, archbishops, bishops and all the clergy and people of East Francia and Bavaria, Bernard, called Abbot of Clairvaux, an abundance of the spirit of valor.

I speak to you of the things of Christ, namely, those wherein lies your salvation. This I say that the authority of the Lord may excuse the unworthiness of the person who speaks — as does also a consideration of desire for you in the love of Jesus Christ. That is now my reason for writing to you, that is the occasion for my venturing to confer with you all by letter. I would prefer to discuss this with you by word of mouth, if only as the will is not lacking so also were the opportunity afforded. "Behold, brothers, now is the accepted time; behold, now is the day of salvation" in full measure. "For the earth shook and trembled" because the God of Heaven begins to lose his land. His land in which he appeared and for more than thirty years went about as a man among men. His land, which he glorified by his miracles, which he consecrated by his own blood, in which the first flowers of the Resurrection appeared. And now, for our sins, the adversaries of the Cross have raised their accursed heads, ravaging with the edge of the sword that blessed land, the land of promise. The time is near, if none stay their hands, when they will burst into the city of the living God, to overthrow the very workshop where our redemption was wrought, to pollute the holy places with the crimson blood of the lamb without spot.

They pant — O the pity of it! — and with sacrilegious jaws for the very shrine of the Christian religion and attempt to profane and to trample underfoot the very resting place wherein for us our Life slumbered in death. What do you, valiant men? What do you, servants of the Cross? Will you thus give that which is holy to the dogs and your pearls to swine? How many sinners there confessing their sins with tears have obtained pardon, since the filthiness of the heathen was eradicated by the swords of our fathers! The Evil One sees this and is envious and gnashes with his teeth and melts away. He stirs the vessels of his iniquity that he may leave no signs or traces of piety if ever — which God forbid — he has the strength to prevail. Truly this is for all ages to come an inconsolable anguish because the loss is irreparable, but to this wicked generation in particular it is an unending source of shame and an eternal reproach. Yet, what think we, brethren? Has the arm of the Lord been shortened or made powerless to save because it summons us little worms to defend and to restore his own inheritance? Can he not send more than twelve legions or even speak the word only and the land shall be free? Surely the power is his whensoever he has the will.

But I say unto you, the Lord your God is making trial of you. He gazes forth over the children of men to see if perchance there is one who understands and makes inquiry and is sorry for him. For God has compassion on his people and provides for those that have fallen low the remedy of salvation. Consider how shrewd a device he employs to save you and marvel; contemplate the depths of his love and have faith, you sinners! He desireth not your death, but that you be converted and live, because he thus seeks an opportunity not against you, but for you. . . .

Happy would I term that generation which obtains the opportunity of so rich an indulgence: a generation which this acceptable year of the Lord, and truly a year of jubilee, finds alive. For this benediction is poured out upon all the world, and all hasten toward this sign of life. Because, therefore, your land is known to be rich in brave men and filled with lusty youth, as your praise is in all the world and the fame of your valor has filled the earth, so gird yourselves also like men and take up your auspicious arms!

Letter 363

Due to disharmony among the leaders, the Second Crusade was a sad failure. In the opening lines of the second book he wrote for Pope Eugene, Bernard offers his theological explanation of this disaster.

We have entered into a period, as you well know, which appears to herald an end almost to our very existence, not to mention our endeavors. Clearly, the Lord, provoked by our sins, seems in some way to have judged the earth before the appointed time, justly, of course, but unmindful of his mercy. He neither spared his people nor his own name. Are they not saying among the nations, "Where is their God?" And no wonder, for the sons of the Church and those who are called by the Christian name lie prostrate in the desert, slain by the sword or destroyed by hunger. Strife has spread among the princes and the Lord makes them wander in trackless wastes. Destruction and misery are in their paths, fear and confusion are in the inner chambers of the kings. How confused are the feet of those announcing peace, of those announcing good news. We said, "Peace" and there is no peace; we promised good news and behold there is disaster as if we were rash or unsure in our endeavor. We rushed into this, not aimlessly but at your command, or rather, through you at God's command. Why, therefore, did we fast and he fail to notice; why did we humble our souls and he ignore us? Indeed, in all of these things his anger is not turned away and his hand is still stretched out. Still how patiently God listens even now to sacrilegious voices and Egyptians blaspheming that he cunningly led them out to die in the wilderness? And yet who does not know that the judgments of the Lord are true? But this judgment is so great an abyss that, in my opinion, he is rightly called blessed who is not shocked by it.

On Consideration, 2.1

He goes on to offer some defense of himself and the Pope who are being denounced and blamed for the failure.

But how does human rashness dare to reprehend what it cannot comprehend? If it is of any consolation, let us remember the judgments of God which are of old. For indeed it is said, "I was mindful of your judgments of old, Lord, and I was comforted." I speak of something formerly known by all but now known by no one. This is exactly how the human heart behaves: what we know when it is not necessary, we forget in time of need. Moses, when he was about to lead the people out of the land of Egypt, promised them a better land. Indeed, for what other reason would this people who knew only one land have followed him? He led them out, but he did not bring them into the land which he had promised. And this sad and unexpected outcome cannot be blamed on the foolhardiness of their leader. He did everything at the Lord's command and with his help and with the Lord confirming his work after with signs. But that people, you say, was stiff-necked and always defying the Lord and his servant Moses. This is true enough; they were unbelieving and rebellious. But what about the people of our day? Ask them? Why do I need to say what they themselves admit? I have one thing to say: How could they advance if they were continually turning back whenever they set out? And when, during their entire journey, did they not return in their hearts to Egypt? If the Israelites fell and perished because of their iniquity, are we astonished that today those who do the same thing suffer the same fate? But was the destruction of the Israelites contrary to the promise of God? Then neither is the destruction of our men. Indeed, the promises of God never impair the justice of God. . . .

Let these few words stand as a defense, so your conscience may have some explanation from me with which it can excuse me and yourself also — if not in the eyes of those who judge actions by their results, certainly in your own eyes. A completely valid excuse for anyone is the testimony of his own conscience. It means nothing to me to be judged by those who call good evil and evil good, who substitute light for darkness and darkness for light. I prefer that the murmuring of the people be against us rather than against God, if a choice must be made. What an honor for me if he deigns to use me for a shield. Willingly I draw to myself the scurrilous tongues of detractors and the poisoned darts of blasphemers so that they do not reach him. I do not refuse to be stripped of glory to prevent an attack on the glory of God.

On Consideration, 2.2-4

Bernard even went on to argue for the resumption of the Crusades, a renewed call to arms on the part of the Pope.

And listen to this. Benjamin sinned. The rest of the tribes armed for vengeance and not without the approval of God. In fact, he appointed the leader for those who were preparing to fight. And so they fought, relying on stronger forces and a more noble cause, and what is greater than all of these, relying on divine favor? But how terrible God is in his counsels over the sons of men. The avengers of the crime fled from the criminals; many fled from a few. But they ran to the Lord and he said to them, "Attack." They attacked again, and again they were scattered in confusion. And so just men went into a just battle, the first time with God's approval and the second time at his command and still they failed. But as they were found inferior in battle, they showed themselves superior in faith. What do you think our men would do with me, if at my urging, they attacked again and were defeated again? When would they listen to me urging them to repeat their march a third time, to repeat the undertaking in which they had already failed a first and a second time? And yet, the Israelites did not think back over their first and second failures, but made preparation for a third time and triumphed. But perhaps our

Facing page:
David Killing the Lion With His Bare Hands (capital). Vézelay.

men are saying, How do we know this message has come from the Lord? What sign do you make that we may believe you? It is not for me to answer these questions; my shame should be spared. You answer for me and for yourself, according to what you have heard and seen, or certainly according to your inspiration from God. . . . Humility restrains me from writing to you that something should be done in this way or that. It is enough that I have intimated that something should be done to console the Church and to close the mouths of those who speak evil.

On Consideration, 2.3-4

In a sermon on the Song of Songs that he wrote at about the same time Bernard spoke more fully of the relationship of the Church to the Jews.

Great is the charity of the Church, who does not begrudge her delight even to her rival, the Synagogue. What could be kinder than to be willing to share with her enemy him whom her soul loves? But it is not surprising, because "salvation is from the Jews."

The Savior returned to the place from which he had come, so that the remnant of Israel might be saved. Let not the branches be ungrateful to the root, nor children to their mother; let not the branches begrudge the roots the sap they took from them nor the children begrudge their mother the milk they sucked from her breast. Let the Church hold fast to the salvation which the Jews lost; we hold it until the fullness of the Gentiles comes and so all Israel may be saved. Let us wish that the universal salvation come to all, for it can be possessed by everyone without anyone having less. This the Church does and more, for we desire for the Jews the name and grace of Bride. This is more than salvation.

On the Song of Songs, 79.5

◆ SIX
At Journey's End

Bernard of Clairvaux arrived at the end of his journey, at Clairvaux, blamed and acclaimed — more acclaimed than blamed — and venerated as a man of God. Already the biography necessary for his canonization had been largely written by his dearest friend, who had preceded him to the grave, William of St. Thierry. Other friends and disciples were also going ahead:

Signs along the pilgrim road, Conques.

Rainard of Cîteaux, Gilbert of Premontre, Suger of St. Denis, and his spiritual son and disciple, Pope Eugene III. But the golden age of Cîteaux was firmly launched. Multitudes of Cistercian abbots would be called upon to lead the churches as bishops. Bernard's successor, Fastrede, the third Abbot of Clairvaux, would with greater ease lead the Order to stand behind Alexander III in the face of an antipope. And the Order would continue to grow and grow.

For almost forty years Bernard had headed his letters "from Bernard, Abbot of Clairvaux." It was how he identified himself. He deeply missed his sons when he was away. He remained close to them in spirit. He dwelt happily in their midst when he was at home. Yet he often experienced the loneliness of the road. In the end, at nine in the morning on August 20, 1153, the Lord granted Bernard his desire and allowed him to close his eyes in death in the midst of his brethren at Clairvaux, his chosen Jerusalem of pilgrimage, the Jerusalem he had created and conceived to be the truest image of the heavenly and eternal Jerusalem to which he now journeyed.

Behind most great men there is a friend, a lover, a woman. Bernard had many friends and freely wrote of his passionate love for them. He had a Lover, and wrote more eloquently of the divine love affair than any who went before him or after him. And he had a Lady, chivalrous knight that he was. The Blessed Virgin Mary was more to him than a Lady. She was Mother, to whom he turned in all his needs: his life, his sweetness, and his hope.

Abbot Bernard deeply loved his spiritual sons and brothers at Clairvaux and sorely missed them when obedience and the needs of the Church took him away from them.

To his dear brethren at Clairvaux, monks, lay brothers and novices, a lasting joy in the Lord, from Brother Bernard.

Your own experience can tell you how much I am suffering. If my absence is irksome to you, you can be sure it is much more so to me. You are suffering from the absence of one person but I am suffering from the absence of each and all of you. And this is something quite different and much harder to bear. I cannot but have as many anxieties as I have sons at Clairvaux; I cannot but fear for the safety and grieve for the absence of each one of you. This twofold grief will never leave me until I am restored to you, for you are part of my life. I have no doubt of what you are feeling for me but I am only one person. You have only one reason for your grief but I have many because I grieve for each of you. It is not only that I am obliged for the time being to live away from you when even to be king would be but a sorry servitude without you but also because I am forced to move in affairs that trouble the peace of my soul and are not very compatible with my vocation.

As you know all this, you ought to

sympathize with me and not be angry at my delay which the needs of the Church renders necessary. Indeed I hope that my presence here may not be necessary for very much longer, but you must pray that it may bring forth fruit. We must reckon as gain the loss we suffer, for it is all in the cause of God. He can easily make good and more than make good what we lose, for he loves us and is all powerful. So we must be of good cheer, for God is with us and no matter how great the distance which seems to separate us we can always be united to each other in him. Any of you who are well disposed, humble, reverent, zealous in reading, attentive in prayer, fervent in fraternal charity can be quite sure I am not far away from you. How could I not be present in spirit to those with whom I am thus united in heart and soul?

Letter 143

In his reluctance to leave his beloved Clairvaux and his community he would at times even make excuses to the Pope.

The letter in which you were good enough to beg me to come to you when you could quite well have ordered me to do so, did not arrive before the feast of the Nativity of Our Blessed Lady. Therefore I do not say I have bought a yoke of oxen or a house or that I have married a wife, but confess quite simply that, as you very well know, I have children and must nourish them. So I do not see how I could come to you without grave scandal and danger to them.
To Pope Innocent II, Letter 152

Bernard's own life as an abbot had been anything if not unusual. His own expansive and universal love along with the demands of others had set him in many directions. To the Carthusians of Portes among whom he had found true friends he wrote:

It is time for me to remember myself. May my monstrous life, my bitter conscience, move you to pity. I am a sort of modern chimaera, neither cleric nor layman. I have kept the habit of a monk but I have long ago abandoned the life. I do not wish to tell you what I dare say you have heard from others: what I am doing, what are my purposes, through what dangers I pass in the world or rather down what precipices I am hurled. If you have not heard, enquire and then, according to what you hear, give your advice and the support of your prayers.
Letter 250

Bernard, who had entered into his sixties, saw his end approaching. To Pope Eugene, who in fact would die six weeks before him, he wrote:

As for myself, your child, I am more feeble than usual. My life ebbs slowly away, drop by drop, probably because I do not deserve a quick death and prompt entry into life.
Letter 270

In time of discouragement and especially as he faced death Bernard was able to turn to his Lady, the Virgin Mother of God. He had an all-embracing devotion to her and had stoutly defended her prerogatives.

There is no doubt that whatever we say in praise of the Mother touches the Son and when we honor the Son we detract nothing from the Mother's glory. For if, as Solomon says, "A wise son is the glory of his father," how much more glorious is it to become the Mother of Wisdom himself? But how can I attempt to praise her whom the prophets have proclaimed, the angel has acknowledged and the evangelist has described as praiseworthy?

In Praise of the Virgin Mother, 4.1

Mary was for him indeed a garden of delights.

Truly may we call Mary a garden of delights, which the divine South Wind not merely comes and blows upon but comes down into and blows through, causing the fragrance of its spices, that is, the precious gifts of heavenly grace to flow out and be spread around on every side. Take away from the sky the sun which enlightens the world and what becomes of the day? Take away Mary, this Star of life's vast and spacious sea, and what is left to us but a cloud of swirling gloom and a thick and dense darkness? Therefore, my brothers, with every fibre of our being, every feeling of our hearts, with all the affections of our minds and with all the ardor of our souls, let us honor Mary because such is the will of God, who would have us obtain everything through her hands. Such I say is the will of God who intends it for our benefit.

Sermon for the Nativity of the Blessed Virgin, 6-7

It was through Mary that Christ himself came to us.

You have already realized, I suppose, that the Virgin herself is the royal road by which the Savior came to us. Therefore, dear brothers and sisters, let us endeavor to ascend by it to Jesus, who by the same way has come down to us. Let us strive, I say, to go by Mary to share his grace who by Mary came to share our misery. Through you, O most Blessed One, Finder of Grace, Mother of Life, Mother of Salvation, through you let us have access to your Son, so that through you he may receive us, he who was given us through you.

Second Sermon for Advent, 5

Mary remains an aqueduct through which Christ's grace comes to us.

Now what is the fountain of life if it be not Christ the Lord? This stream from the heavenly source descends to us through an aqueduct. It does not show all the fullness of the fountain, but it moistens our dry and withered hearts with some few drops of grace, giving more to one, less to another. The aqueduct is always full, so that all may receive of its fullness.

You must have already guessed, dear brothers, to whom I allude under the image of an aqueduct, which receiving the fullness of the Fountain from the Father's heart has passed it on to us, at least in so far as we can contain it. You know it was she to whom it was said, "Hail, full of grace."

But how did this Aqueduct of ours attain to the loftiness of the Fountain? How indeed, except by the ardor of her desires, by the fervor of her devotion, by the purity of her prayer? How did she reach up even to the inaccessible Majesty but by knocking, by asking, by seeking? And she found what she was seeking, since it was said to her: "You have found favor with God."

Sermon for the Nativity of the Blessed Virgin, 6

"And the Virgin's name was Mary." In speaking of Mary, Bernard's prose turned poetic. We have here one of his finest.

Facing page: Virgin and Child. One of the most famous Cistercian thirteenth-century sculptures, Fontenay.

Let us now say a few words about this name [Stella Maris], which means "star of the sea" and is so becoming the Virgin Mother. Surely she is very fittingly likened to a star. . . . O you, whoever you are, who feel in the tidal wave of this world you are nearer to being tossed about among the squalls and gales than treading on dry land, if you do not want to founder in the tempest, do not avert your eyes from the brightness of the star. When the wind of temptation blows up within you, when you strike upon the rock of tribulation, gaze up at the star, call out to Mary. Whether you are being tossed about by the waves of pride or ambition or slander or jealousy, gaze up at this star, call out to Mary. When rage or greed or fleshly desires are battering the skiff of your soul, gaze up at Mary. When the immensity of your sins weighs you down and you are bewildered by the loathsomeness of your conscience, when the terrifying thought of judgment appalls you and you begin to founder in the gulf of sadness and despair, think of Mary. In dangers, in hardships, in every doubt, think of Mary, call out to Mary. Keep her in your mouth, keep her in your heart. Follow the example of her life and you will obtain the favor of her prayer. Following her you will never go astray. Asking her help, you will never despair. Keeping her in your thoughts, you will never wander away. With your hand in hers, you will never stumble. With her protecting you, you will not be afraid. With her leading you, you will never tire. Her kindness will see you through to the end. Then you will know from your own experience how true it is that "the Virgin's name was Mary."

In Praise of the Virgin Mother, 2.17

The words Bernard sent to the monks in Ireland on the occasion of the death of St. Malachy at Clairvaux not only convey his own attitude toward death but can be applied by us to Bernard's own passing.

If we had here an abiding city we might rightly shed many tears at the loss of such a fellow citizen. But if we look, as we should, for the one that is to come, the loss of such a valuable elder will still be an occasion of sorrow, yet in this case knowledge should moderate our feelings and sure hope set a limit to our grief. It ought to be no surprise if our affection wrings a groan from our hearts, if our sense of bereavement expresses itself in tears, yet there should be a measure to our grief. We should in fact find some consolation for it in the contemplation not of what we can see but of what we cannot see. We must be glad for the sake of this holy soul, otherwise he would accuse us in the words of our Lord to the Apostles, "If you really loved me you would be glad to hear that I am on my way to my Father."

The spirit of our father has gone ahead of us to the Father of the world of the spirits. We would prove ourselves not only wanting in charity but also ungrateful for all that we have received through him, were we not glad for his sake that he has passed from his many labors to everlasting repose, from the dangers of the world to the safety of heaven, from the world to the Father. It is an act of filial piety to grieve for the death of Malachy, but it were an act of even greater filial piety to rejoice with him in the life that he has found. Has he not found life? Surely he has and a blessed life. In the eyes of fools he seemed to die, but all is well with him.

Even consideration of our own advantage suggests that we should rejoice and be glad that we have such a powerful patron in the court of heaven, a faithful advocate whose deep love will not permit him to forget us and whose well-tried holiness will obtain for him the favor of God. Who would dare to believe that the holy Malachy loves his sons and daughters less now or is less able to help them than he was? There is no doubt that since God loved him before he died he now enjoys a deeper and more sure experience of God's love, and that since he loved his own, he loved them to the end.

May it be far from us, O holy Soul, to consider your prayers less helpful to us now that you are offering them to the Divine Majesty with even greater eagerness, now that you are no longer living by faith but reigning by vision! Far may it be from us to believe that your charity is in any way less active than it was now that you sit at the very font of charity and are able to draw deep draughts of it instead of the drops for which you used to thirst.

Charity is strong and cannot yield to death, it is even stronger than death.

I exhort you, my brethren, to follow carefully in the footsteps of our father, all the more zealously for knowing from daily experience his holy way of life. You will prove yourself his true sons by manfully keeping his teaching. As you saw in him and received from him a pattern of how you ought to live, live by that pattern, and make more of it than ever. "Wise sons are the pride of their father."
Letter 374

Epilogue

We have in the course of the preceding pages gotten some glimpses, obscured somewhat by a lot of powerful and colorful rhetoric, into the mind and heart of Bernard of Clairvaux, a man of God who never ceased to be a man, passionate and passionately concerned. Like most of us, he was prone to identify what he thought to be right to be actually and unquestionably right. And being the God-centered and theological person that he was, he was also prone to identify what he saw to be right to be right according to God — to be the will of God. Thus the pursuit of it harnessed all his passionate love for God. Perhaps he was too prone to see things black and white, or at least to paint them this way in his vibrant and moving discourse.

But what really made Bernard the powerful person he was, the attractive person who drew the hearts of so many, the man whose memory has stood the test of time?

When we are young and starting out on the road to greatness and power we often have recourse to others. We find our power in being connected with those who truly possess power and influence. If by close association with them we can in some way influence them and their decisions we feel we are making a difference. As we grow we are not content with this but want ourselves to be the ones who make the decisions and determine the course of events. As we further mature we seek to extend our power and influence through the gathering of followers, adherents, or disciples. Through them our influence reaches out to more distant places and more varied areas of life.

Finally, as we age we become more concerned about how we will live on in the memory of those who come after, how we will remain a presence that will make a difference even after we ourselves have completed this mortal journey. These are the elements of greatness and power: connection and influence, decisive leadership, followers, and a lasting effective presence.

We find all of them certainly very present in the life of Bernard of Clairvaux. If he lived today he would be the person who could get right through to the president, the prime ministers, the Pope himself. No secretary would hold up the call. Letters from him would receive personal attention. Bernard had ready access to all the great personages of his time. In his own sphere, which was his chosen sphere — he refused more than one miter — his was the decisive voice. He took the vision of the founders of the Cistercian Order — in fact he was one with them in the actual founding of that Order as an order — and gave it a theological expression and practical implementation, establishing it in almost every corner of the Christian world. From the very first moment when the Cistercian ideal became his own he began to gather co-adherents in a way that astonishes us. I can just picture myself trying to get my brother to send his wife and children to a nunnery so that he could come with me to the monastery! Not every candidate arrives at the gate of the abbey with thirty relatives and friends in tow. The stories of Bernard's magnetic drawing power are numerous. It is said that when he spoke to the students at Paris half of them left the schools to enter upon the monastic way. What is a fact is that Bernard in the course of forty years founded or adopted sixty-eight monasteries, which in turn founded many more, even while he fostered the foundation and growth of hundreds of other monasteries in the Cistercian federation. His disciples, like him, took up the pen and left rich and beautiful expressions of the same spiritual heritage. They, like him, wielded considerable political and social influence in their respective areas. They filled many episcopal thrones and ascended to the papal throne. And his influence lives on. Today, nine centuries later, millions hold his name in benediction and annually celebrate his feast. Churches, monasteries, schools, and other centers of learning and social outreach bear his name in many parts of the world. Several hundred monasteries are populated by women and men who look to him as a living spiritual father. And new Cistercian communities are being founded every year.

Bernard is then a powerful man, even a great man. But what made him such an attractive man? Maybe it was that he was also a flawed man, and yet this did not prevent him from being a totally vibrant person with an enlivening vision that gave endless passion to his life and offered this vibrancy to others. At the end of his life Bernard did not speak of his power or his greatness or influence. In the last of his formal writings — the last of the five books called *On Consideration* and the last of the sermons on the Song of Songs that he composed — he spoke of God, the Transcendent, and of intimate union with him. In his more personal writing he spoke of human misery, need, and friendship.

Bernard is a man of paradox. He goes to an obscure, relatively new little monastery seeking a humble, hidden life of prayer and obedience, yet he is a leader — he draws a whole entourage with him. He is a writer — his pen cannot be still and his writings are instant best-sellers. He is a passionate lover — and his love harnesses all his forces in almost driven service of the One he loves and the programs that he believes that One wants. He always aspired to contemplation, yet till his death he was one of the most active leaders of his times. When he comes to write about humility he eloquently and extensively describes pride. His one strictly theological treatise struggles with the most profound of human paradoxes: human freedom and the effective prevenient grace of God. He would have knights become monks and yet remain knights in the creation of a whole new type of religious order, the Knights Templar. He would have a monk Pope and still remain at heart a monk. He was a man of peace, yet he eloquently and effectively called forth the civil arm to wield the sword. For those who look at him from without, Bernard is a bundle of contradictions. For those who seek to look at him from within there is some hope that they might get an intuitive glimpse at how it all held together for him and in that perhaps find a key to bringing together the paradoxes within their own lives.

For Bernard Jesus Christ was the

"saving link." He who brought together in his own being God and human, each remaining whole and integral, undiminished in its allness. For Bernard the key concept was *modus*: harmonious balance, a mean without mediocrity. Extremes remain, whole and undiminished in their power, yet united in their goal and ultimate meaning. If indeed all that is comes forth from God and returns to God, then all must have a unity. And "where unity is, there is perfection." For Bernard these were not abstract concepts. He lived them. He incorporated into his life apparently irreconcilable extremes. And lesser persons saw it that way and continue to see it that way. But for him and for anyone who through the type of contemplation he teaches comes to unity with the center, with God the source and the end, the paradoxes resolve themselves in unity and peace.

Bernard spoke of his times as *tempora periculosa*: "Dangers are no longer imminent, they are present." We can identify with this. And this gave an urgency to his idealism. Like the best of us he was socially and politically concerned. "Everywhere the powerful oppress the poor. We cannot abandon the downtrodden; we cannot refuse judgment to those who suffer injustice," he wrote to the Pope. Like each of us, he had limited physical resources and, though extraordinarily endowed, limited intellectual resources also. He used them as best he could, trying to discern the leadings of the Lord. He drew on the unlimited spiritual resources that are available to us all and pushed a frail and abused body to a heroic service. He created masterful pieces of literature even while engaged in extensive political and administrative activity. It is only those who meditate regularly and draw on that same spiritual reserve who can understand how he could do this.

Here, too, I believe, is the secret of this flawed man's immense attractiveness. His weakness and very humanness brought him close to his fellows. They could identify with him, compassionate with him, even pity him. And they could find hope in him. For if even this poor struggling human, weighed down as he was by infirmity, was able to burn with the spark of life, fight indefatigably for a cause that is right, and reach out to the Divine and hope for transcendent union, then who could not do the same? Our problem lies in the fact that a misguided hagiography sought to strip Bernard of all his humanness, hide his flaws, and present an ideal too lofty for us poor humans to identify with. The real Bernard who is hidden beneath the halo, the Church, the crosier, and the cowl is very much our brother, our fellow human. He knew deeply in his bones the weariness of human life. Yet he also knew to reach into the center of his being where dwells a Divine Force and to draw upon that Force, that Force he came to know as Love. A Divine Love enabled a flawed human to become himself an eminently powerful and attractive force.

Bernard of Clairvaux is a man who, without ceasing to be a man, became a man of God.

CHRONOLOGY

1090 — Bernard is born at Fontaines-les-Dijon in Burgundy.
1098 — Robert of Molesme with his prior Alberic, subprior Stephen, and nineteen others found Cîteaux, March 21.
1103 — Bernard's mother, Aleth, dies.
1109 — Alberic dies and Stephen becomes Abbot of Cîteaux.
1112 — Bernard enters Cîteaux with thirty relatives and friends.
1115 — Bernard founds Clairvaux with twelve other monks.
1118 — Bernard sends his first group from Clairvaux to found Trois Fontaines. By the time of Bernard's death Clairvaux would have sixty-eight affiliations.
1118 — Bernard is isolated from the community for a year.
1119 — Bernard's father, Tescelin, enters Clairvaux shortly before his death. Pope Calixtus II confirms the *Carta Caritatis*.
1123 — Bernard publishes his first work, *In Praise of the Virgin Mary*.
1124 — Bernard writes *The Steps of Humility and Pride* for Abbot Godfrey of Langres, Abbot of Fontenay.
1125 — Bernard writes his *Apologia* for William of St. Thierry.
1126 — Cardinal Haimeric is named chancellor of the Holy Roman Church for whom Bernard writes *On Loving God*.
1128 — Synod of Troyes is held. Bernard promotes the approbation of the Knights of the Temple and writes for them *In Praise of the New Knighthood*.
1128 — Bernard writes *On Grace and Free Will* for William of St. Thierry.
1130 — Election of Innocent II and an antipope. Bernard works eight years to heal this schism.
1131 — Pope Innocent II visits Clairvaux.
1132 — Bernard sends a group of monks to found Rievaulx in England.
1133 — Bernard enters Rome with Innocent II. Lothair is crowned emperor.
1134 — Abbot Stephen Harding of Cîteaux dies.
1135 — Council of Pisa. Excommunication of the antipope.
1135 — Bernard begins his sermons on the Song of Songs. He will complete eighty-six sermons in this series before his death.
1137 — Louis VII becomes King of France.
1138 — End of the papal schism. Conrad III becomes emperor.
1139 — Malachy, Archbishop of Armagh, comes to Clairvaux. Later he will return to die in his friend's arms. Nine years later, in 1148, Bernard writes his *Life of Saint Malachy*.
1140 — Bernard speaks to the clerics at Paris and then writes *On the Conversion of Clerics*.
1140 — Council of Sens. Condemnation of Peter Abelard. Bernard writes *Against the Errors of Peter Abelard*.
1143 — Bernard responds to two Benedictines with *On Precepts* and *Dispensations*.
1145 — Bernard's spiritual son is elected Pope Eugene III.
1146 — Bernard begins to preach the Second Crusade at Vézelay. Bernard defends the Jews in the Rhineland. Diet of Spires is convened.
1147 — Pope Eugene III visits Clairvaux.
1149 — Bernard begins his five books entitled *On Consideration* for Pope Eugene III.
1153 — Bernard dies at Clairvaux, August 20.
1174 — Bernard is canonized by Pope Alexander III, January 18.

SELECT BIBLIOGRAPHY

Bernard of Clairvaux, *The Works of Bernard of Clairvaux*, tr. Michael Casey et. al. (Spencer, MA; Kalamazoo, MI: Cistercian Publications, 1969-).
The Letters of St. Bernard of Clairvaux, tr. Bruno Scott James (London: Burns Oates, 1953).
Casey, Michael, *Athirst for God: Spiritual Desire in Bernard of Clairvaux's Sermons on the Song of Songs*, Cistercian Studies Series 77 (Kalamazoo, MI: Cistercian Publications, 1987).
Cristiani, Leon, *St. Bernard of Clairvaux*, tr. M. Angeline Bouchard (Boston, MA: St. Paul Editions, 1977).
Daniel-Rops, Henri, *Bernard of Clairvaux*, tr. Elizabeth Abbott (New York: Hawthorn, 1964).
Diemer, Paul, *Love Without Measure: Extracts From the Writings of St. Bernard of Clairvaux* (Kalamazoo, MI: Cistercian Publications, 1990).
Evans, G. R., *The Mind of St. Bernard of Clairvaux* (Oxford: Clarendon Press, 1983).
Gilson, Étienne, *The Mystical Theology of Saint Bernard*, tr. A.H.C. Downes (Kalamazoo, MI: Cistercian Publications, 1990).
Hufgard, M. Kilian, *Saint Bernard of Clairvaux: A Theory of Art Formulated from his Writings and Illustrated in Twelfth-Century Works of Art*, Mediaeval Studies 2 (Lewiston, NY: Edwin Mellen Press, 1989).
Leclercq, Jean, *A Second Look at Saint Bernard*, Cistercian Studies Series 105 (Kalamazoo, MI: Cistercian Publications, 1990).
Merton, Thomas, *The Last of the Fathers* (New York: Harcourt Brace & World, 1954). This volume includes a translation of Pope Pius XII's encyclical *Mellifluus Doctor*.
Pennington, M. Basil, *Last of the Fathers: The Cistercian Fathers of the Twelfth Century* (Still River, MA: St. Bede's, 1983).
Pennington, M. Basil, ed., *Saint Bernard of Clairvaux: Studies Commemorating the Eighth Centenary of his Canonization*, Cistercian Studies Series 28 (Kalamazoo, MI: Cistercian Publications, 1977).
William of St. Thierry, *St. Bernard of Clairvaux*, tr. Geoffrey Webb and Adrian Walker (Westminster, MD: Newman, 1960).